NOT MY PLAN

Sucking it in Until I Had To Push it Out

*Allie -
Hope you enjoy
my story! [signature]*

MEGAN BRYANT

NOT MY PLAN

Sucking it in Until I Had To Push it Out

Megan Bryant

Editorial Work by AnnaMarie McHargue

Cover Design by Aaron Snethen

Interior Design by Aaron Snethen

ISBN (print): 9781945537004
ISBN (ebook): 9781945537035

Printed in the United States of America.

Dedicated to Hannah

Within this life, nothing else can compare,
To being captured in a newborn's stare.

True devotion forged deep within the heart,
Mere moments together, too soon we part.

Trial of virtue, urged maturity,
To make the choice for your security.

No more a child, responsibility,
Setting forth a lifelong trajectory.

Tiny package, of love and labor born,
Gifted to empty arms, no longer mourn.

Beyond this mortal life, connection span,
This monumental task was not my plan.

INTRODUCTION

"To everything there is a season, and a time for every purpose under the heaven."
Ecclesiastes 3:1

Simple enough!

While I agree with this statement, I must confess that I struggle with its practical application. For example, I always thought, "One day, if only for posterity's sake, I'll write down my story about the time I hid an entire pregnancy." Now, if I would have known that the timing in which it would feel most critical would be when I was a mother to three young children, "working" from home struggling to keep my head above water financially as I chase my dreams as a performer, and being swept up in the seemingly endless typhoon of emotions that accompany the biggest marital challenges so far in my 15-year effort (a different story for a different book), I'd have said, "Thanks, but no thanks."

Good news. I'm a comedian. What an advantage to be able to laugh away my cares, right? I know what you are already saying in your mind: "Oh good, this is going to be hilarious! Tell me a joke."

No. I will not. This is neither the time nor the place, but hopefully some of my whimsical and humorous ways will bleed out onto these pages as I share this true story of mine. And, I'm confident that a decade or so from now, I'll look back on this chaotic time in my life, wondering how in the Sam-hay I got anything done, and breathe a well-deserved sigh of relief.

For many years, I kept my story fairly guarded, only sharing with a few select people here and there when I felt it was appropriate. Early on, it was mostly because I felt bad that I had become a statistic. I was a little worried about being judged, although, it was mostly because I didn't want the beautiful transaction of adoption I had just gone through to be overshadowed by anyone else's opinion. No one else was there through my experience. True, the birth father knew, and I think he believed he was supporting me the best that he could, but no one, not even he, could be inside my heart and mind throughout that process.

So, why unearth this experience that is such an important part of my long-distant past? So much has happened during the past 16 years. Why should I be telling this story now?

In comedy, if you get your timing right, a well-told joke can unite the audience in both laughter and solidarity. With stand-up there is a certain amount of risk you are taking as well. Just because your material may not resonate with everyone in the room, it doesn't mean you can't still have a fun time together. If I've learned anything in comedy, it's that you have to be yourself and understand that not everyone will like you. BUT, if you are true to yourself, no one can argue with that and there is a far greater appreciation for your authenticity.

Timing for something like this book can only be partially planned; you just have to take a leap of faith that it will all work out. I'm at that place in my life now, standing on the precipice, bending my knees in preparation for the jump.

The thoughts about when to open the gates of my private life for inevitable scrutiny have been stirring in my soul for a long time.

When spring 2015 rolled around, I was swamped with life's usual overwhelm. Now, a year later, I'm home with my three young children, trying to build a personal empire in the entertainment business from Boise, Idaho, which is no small feat. I gave birth to my youngest child in January 2015 and, for the first time, I didn't have to return to my day job to punch someone else's time clock.

A few short months later, in April, I was featured in two local magazines for my success with community events and "ditching" the day job to *pursue my dreams.* As I read the articles about myself, I felt this bizarre twinge in my mind that this word picture painted about me was far too simple. As if the world just yielded to my whim and allowed me to dance playfully on the surface. There was no mention of my personal struggle to become the woman I am today.

Is this what people think of me? A mom in a picture-perfect family? Not a care in the world while success just smiles on me, somehow dodging the bullets of life, and coasting from one awesome adventure to the next?

I can barely stand to read these articles. I see some of my own quotes and feel ashamed. "…Many comics struggle with depression and are absolutely miserable. There's a dark side with many comedians, who are really absorbed by their own problems," I said in one magazine. I stand by this statement, but the point that gets missed a lot is that when I speak about comics as a general term, I'm including myself in the equation. *I'm one of the comics*. For some reason it still comes across that I have somehow bypassed the heartache, when really, I'm in the trenches with them.

I don't complain a lot, and certainly not publicly, and no, most of my material isn't rant-based or woe-is-me, but that doesn't mean I haven't clung to the craft of comedy for the exact same reasons that countless others have. I've used the stage as a way to cope with my trials and to seek out validation from others. I'm a master at using laughter to mask the pains of my world.

I was sick of being that person who only posts super positive stuff on Facebook. It felt like it was finally time to be completely real with people, but in a way that would be relatable. Hey guys! I'm a huge mess and riding on an emotional pendulum that just won't quit swinging, so let's just get together and all hug it out.

I was going through the worst bout of post-partum depression I'd ever experienced. I like to blame it on the baby, who was a week late and nearly 11 pounds. He stayed stuck posterior for a good portion of the labor and delivery until my doctor-turned-farmhand went in to her elbow to flip him over, finally dislodging his royal giantness from my mangled guts. The reality is, outside the delivery room, I was simultaneously embarking on some heavy marital issues. Not new ones, just the same old unattended and festering issues that had plagued our entire marriage. I spilt my literal and figurative guts that day, and that was the beginning of the newest edition of myself. I became Megan Bryant, False Image Destroyer.

Now, in this heightened, frenzied mental state, feeling much like an abandoned single parent, my tired heap of a woman sunk into a chaotic mental state that felt like what I imagine tripping on acid to be like. Immediately after delivery, all of my senses were at 17 on the 10 scale.I felt I could actually hear danger brewing. It was as if every hair on my body was an antenna, receiving infinite signals of desperation from the far reaches of the planet. My husband might be home physically, but his mind was always elsewhere, and the thought of voluntarily helping or providing comfort to me wasn't on his radar.

If I managed to step outside for a moment of fresh air, I would stare intently at each house on my street and wonder what was happening behind closed doors. What if my neighborhood was harboring a fugitive? A drug lord? A pedophile? What if there was a child being held against his will at this very moment on this very street? How could I initiate a rescue mission? I could feel everything that was wrong in the world, and I swear I could even see germs floating through the air in Technicolor.

Every waking moment I worried that my children would choke on something, anything, and die. Bookshelves were waiting to spring from the walls and crush my babies. Packing them up to go to the grocery store felt like a tactical operation, prepping to go to war. Each time I put the key in the ignition to turn on the Jeep, I would hold my breath, and squint my eyes, wincing, as I expected the whole thing to blow up into a fireball right there in the garage, or the parking lot, or even sometimes while sitting idle at the stoplight.

Anything bad that could happen, COULD really happen. And I, in some moments, wanted to be brave and prepare for it. In other moments, I just wanted to drift into an eternal sleep and never have to think of it, or anything, ever again.

I was aware enough to understand that these thoughts were completely crazy, which led me to believe I wasn't actually crazy. As I gradually regained composure after about six months, I felt like it was time to stop trying to uphold this image of the perfect, flawless, impossible life and be real. I stood up, loud and proud, happy to share my life with others and trust that some people out there could relate and would find comfort in knowing they weren't the only ones lost in a personal pandemonium.

When I went public with my story in September 2015, I was flooded with Facebook likes, and private messages from friends and church members who were so apologetic for not being there for me. They were so thoughtful and I enjoyed reconnecting with them. Many of them said that if they had known, they would have been there for me. While that may be true, it is much easier to say so 16 years later. But thinking back, when I was in the thick of it, I wouldn't have had any idea which people to pick out for a chat. And, I really can't imagine that I would have let anyone get too close to the situation anyway. I had battened down the hatches and hid myself away from the world.

When I think about all the "what if's," it truly scares me. If I had let people in on the situation, would my choice have been influenced one way or another? Would I have leaned too much on other people to make decisions for me? I don't know. I like to think it would have all worked out regardless, but I'm not so sure it would have. With the way it did happen I was able to remain in control of the choices and steer myself down the path that I felt was right without having loud, well-intentioned voices of opinion clouding my decision.

I don't blame anyone for any of this. So many people said how sorry they were that they didn't know, that they didn't support me. But I have never once felt anger toward anyone for not being there. To me, it was a decision I had to face alone.

Likewise, I've never harbored regret for the path I chose, but I do regret not addressing it with friends earlier so they could know it was okay. Everything is okay. We are all okay.

Over the past few years the media has been swamped with the topic of abortion, and particularly with regard to the controversies around Planned Parenthood. What always strikes me is how callously the topic is discussed. My personal experience at Planned Parenthood back in May 1999 was the source of a major plot element in my unplanned pregnancy. It seems as though an unplanned or unwanted pregnancy is met with two options; terminate, or keep the baby to raise yourself. Very infrequently do I see a light shine on the third—and very viable option—placing the baby for adoption.

I am an advocate for adoption, but even more than that, I am an advocate for ensuring that women have all the information regarding ALL the options available to those with an unplanned pregnancy. It is only with all of the information that a woman can confidently make the decision she will have to live with every single day for the rest of her life.

I'm also an advocate for speaking YOUR truth, whatever that is. Some mistakes or sins we commit are easier to hide than others, but, at the root, we are all just clumsy humans trying to make sense of it all. I believe that through our experiences we can achieve personal greatness if we take the time to learn as we go, and to find opportunities to extend our hand from time to time to help someone else out of the trenches they have inadvertently stepped into.

So, here we are. What an honor it is for my words to be flowing into your brain juices at this very moment. Thank you for taking time out of your life to read this book. And thanks in advance for buying many, many more copies to give to everyone you know. I'm sure you can already sense this will make a great gift.

CHAPTER 1
In the Spotlight

House lights dim. Spotlight cuts through the darkness and illuminates the stage, catching dust particles in its trail that glitter and swirl, moved by the ceiling fans overhead. I can feel the audiences' energy as they shift in their seats, sip their drinks, and finish up the conversation they are having with their friends with a hurried, loud-whispered statement.

As a comic, stepping into that spot of light I transcend into another world. I can say and do anything I want. A captive audience has no choice but to listen, but will they really hear me?

As the performance unfolds, that sweet, delicious moment comes when the room floods with laughter because of something I've said or some kooky face I've made. I crave that sound of release. It gives me validation. This is my safe place. I feel untouchable. I can't get enough so I keep working for the next laugh. When a joke hits an audience just right, and strikes that magical chord in the room, there is nothing more satisfying. I know in those moments, those people are laughing at me and laughing with me. I live for those brief wrinkles in time when, through the power of laughter, we exhale all the burdens we are carrying.

Every time I take the stage, it is like an airplane ride. "This is your captain speaking," I think to myself. The visual helps me to take control and accountability for our adventure together. I care about every soul. Everyone buckled into seats locked in their upright and most uncomfortable position. Engines on, we are picking up speed as I utter my first line. "I ate a lot of cat food as a child..." and we have lift off.

Not every flight is perfect. Many of them are bumpy along the way, but we are in it together, one way or another. When a set goes perfectly, we are all onboard smiling, comfortable and collected, sipping on ginger ale. When a set bombs, everyone reaches for the barf bags.

Just like a flight to anywhere, every passenger boarded that plane for a different reason. Maybe for a vacation, or, perhaps, just a business trip. For a world traveler this may be the first of several connecting flights. Maybe there is a new baby across the country, and an eager grandmother heads to snuggle new life. In the very next aisle another passenger heading to attend a funeral, saying goodbye to a life ended. Yet, they all file into the fuselage with their destination in mind, trusting the pilot and crew will get them there safely.

Before every show I scan the room and watch people. I'm curious about their differences. I let my mind race a bit. Why are they here? What was their day like? Are they happy or feigning a smile to save face with friends? Are they celebrating something tonight? Are they trying to escape something that is troubling them? Did they choose to be here or did someone drag them along for a night of comedy? How can I connect with them? Will they like me? Whatever the reason, they are here now and I have a job to do.

It is no small undertaking to step onto a stage and make people laugh. For me, it is especially difficult if there are a lot of women in the crowd. They are going to judge my clothes, hair, and make-up. I can see their arms crossed and that look on their face that tells me I better be funny or else. Even when I'm rockin' sneakers, jeans, and a cardigan from Target, they close off a little bit and check to make sure their boyfriends don't laugh at me. I open with something that lets them know that I'm just a goofy gal trying to figure life out, too, and once the ladies are on my team, we can all laugh together.

Sometimes in conversation or during interviews I find myself explaining that comedians are very damaged people. That they, WE, have experienced things in life that we somehow feel compelled to share. I used to think that comics were a rare breed of folks who really have gone through the ringer in life, suffering greater tragedies than most other people, and, sadly, many were hardened to the world. And, that is absolutely the truth, in most cases, of who they are. However, during recent years I've finally come to the happy realization that we are *all* damaged people. Comics just happen to have enough reckless abandon to broadcast their life for all to hear.

Comics have a grasp on life at an elevated level. Of course, they see the hurt in the world and embrace the insanity of all the tragedy that surrounds them. They tackle the social chaos that still runs rampant around politics, gender stereotypes, and religion. They head straight into the fire of topics like mental illness, abuse, homelessness, rape, abortion, alcoholism, racism, autism, and every other kind of ism you can think of. They see the humor in the stupid things people say and do. They call attention to those pet peeves that we can all relate to. They embrace the madness and use comedy as a tool to connect with people so we can all, collectively, deal with our crap.

But let me be clear: Talking and making light of serious issues does not mean the issue itself is funny, or that the comedian is intentionally making fun of people. (Well, sometimes they are, but, by and large, that isn't what fuels them.) Sometimes people just want to get offended and talk about how inappropriate comedy is. In reality it can and should be viewed as a powerful tool to create a stir around sensitive subjects. And guess what, if it makes you uncomfortable, that is a good thing because it's probably an important topic.

Comedy helps to level the playing field. Real issues and observations are put on display in front of a live audience, and when it resonates with people, that's where the connection begins.

Comics, especially the really great ones, can take these topics and make them palpable. They are some of the bravest people I've ever met. Few jobs allow you to talk with blunt truth and not freak out all of your co-workers or get yourself fired. Trust me, I get it, for 10 years I worked in retail banking where I was encouraged to leave my personal life at the door so I could get my work done.

Spending so much time around comedians and getting to know their backgrounds, I'm always amazed at their endurance and bravery, their faith and determination. There are some very dark stories out there, and I know that many countless stories of heartbreak are in the world all around me. Is it any wonder that there are so many people who question the very existence of a God? I don't pretend to have all the answers. I've struggled with my faith on more than one occasion and probably will again in the future. Yet, somehow, through these trials there is a transition point where renewal is possible. Connecting with humanity and embracing the humor in our circumstances can aid in the healing.

So why did I become a comic? To be honest I didn't deliberately seek it out. I didn't know how. I loved to perform and make people laugh, but to embark on a career in comedy just did not fit into my plan. I had grown up with private daydreams of moving to Hollywood and becoming famous. In the back of my mind, I always felt like I was already at a disadvantage. I didn't have tons of formal training in music and acting. I took the classes available through public school and was at a decent talent level, but not at a get-all-the-solos-and-lead-roles level like I thought I needed to become a wildly rich, brilliant actor. Plus, I'm from Boise, Idaho, and global connectivity through things like MySpace, YouTube, and Facebook were still years down the road.

My introduction to becoming a comic came in two unexpected phases. Once, when my older brother invited me to an improv practice with a bunch of people in someone's living room on a sunny Saturday morning in 2006, and the other when I was innocently watching an open mic for stand-up comedy, and in 2010 when, with zero warning, the host called me up as the next comic. In both cases I had the cliché "aha" moments where my destiny began to fall into place. I could do comedy performances right in my hometown, fitting them into my busy lifestyle, and making them whatever I wanted them to be.

While that technical structure may have occurred to me in my 20s, I've been a performer my whole life. As a young child I would sing non-stop and create little jingles for everything I saw.

I talked to myself constantly. I'd record myself on a cassette tape as both the interviewer and the interviewee discussing the premier of my new movie, or album release, or philanthropic adventure. I still talk to myself.

In 2011, my day job (as a Project Manager for Volunteer Firefighter Recruitment and Retention Initiatives, using funding through FEMA programs and the Department of Homeland Security) had me traveling all over the country, and when work was done, I would track down the comedy clubs and work on my material, making new friends along the way.

In 2012, I wanted to stretch my ambitious legs in my hometown by creating an annual comedy festival. I got right to work assembling a big celebration of comedy called, "Idaho Laugh Fest." I have an abundance of comedy friends and acquaintances now, and my favorite thing about them is their rawness and determination to be the boldest version of themselves. They have endured so much. They are broken people. What I love about those comics is that it's BECAUSE of those painful experiences, those truths in their own lives, that they become relatable. They become heroes on the stage for exposing their insecurities before a live audience.

I've learned over the years that people expect me to be the happy ray of sunshine and giggles they can turn to if they are having a bad day, so, in my own circles, I was made to feel like a big deal. For many years, I told myself that needed to be enough.

I liked being that person, but it is really hard to keep that smile on my face all day, every day, year after year. And don't get me wrong, I enjoy being the person who makes people laugh and feel good about themselves, but I finally got tired of everyone thinking I'm happy-go-lucky because I've never known sorrow or trials.

When my personal life took a jolting turn off the straight and narrow during my senior year of high school, I thought all my dreams were over. Any hope of following a performer's ambition took the bench and I chose a safe, responsible route by securing a respectable day job. I had grown up with a good work ethic, earning my own money for extracurricular activities and drivers-ed. I felt compelled, in a whirlwind of rectifying a challenging situation, to take the road of caution and stability.

I made an irresponsible decision that resulted in an unplanned pregnancy. That's where this story begins.

In small doses I've shared with people my story of adoption, and other harrowing experiences, and there is a moment of shock as they digest the reality that, in spite of all the outward appearances, I am not immune to struggle. Trust me, people, I've been to the edge, and I've wanted to drive my Jeep over that edge.

I'm not famous. Sometimes I feel like my story would have a greater impact if I were famous. If I had some credibility. Why would anyone want to read a book about this Mormon girl from Boise, Idaho who got knocked up in high school and stumbled upon adoption at the last possible minute? The truth is, there will be a lot of people who won't care. That's fine. But I know that this experience has been the most pivotal event in my life. It made me question everything. It made me face my own mortality and broaden my capacity to navigate this crazy life while I'm still here.

For years I kept this to myself, except for very close acquaintances. There is a weird, judgy stigma around adoption and I just don't like to voluntarily put myself in a position to receive that judgment. Often times, people probably don't even realize how rudely they are coming across. Even now, when I share small parts of my story, or mention that I'm a birth mom, some people will say, "Oh! I could NEVER do that. I could never give away my baby! I just love them so much, and I just COULD. NOT. DO IT."

Yeah, I get what you are saying, lady, but you aren't helping anyone. Trust me, I know love. I love my three young children more than I even realized was possible. And guess what. I love my first-born daughter, who I placed for adoption, with that same intense love. I love her more and more as time goes on, and I loved her so much that I remember the indescribable emotion sweeping over me the moment I laid eyes on her. I loved her when I could feel her moving inside me, my guts like a jungle gym.

I loved her so much that I absolutely had to put her first. I had to put aside the feelings of heartache that I would have to endure in order to make the RIGHT decision for HER. It wasn't about me anymore. I could have made it work. I could have been "responsible" and married her birth father and lived in his parent's basement. The offer was on the table. My own parents could have helped raise her. Somehow it could have worked out, but, in my heart, I knew that wasn't the path I should take.

My decision was 100 percent about her. I loved her so much that I wanted her to have a mom and dad and a sister in a home that was ready for a baby. I wanted her to have everything I wasn't capable of giving her at that time in my life.

Several years after I'd settled into my typical adult life, I knew there was something more for me. My kooky personality belonged on the stage. It became my humble obligation to help spread joy and laughter, even for seconds at a time, and share my raw and real understanding of the world in a way that gives hope to others. I don't take the spotlight for granted. In fact, I feel a strong sense of responsibility to use that time wisely. To give everything I can to the craft of entertaining people in a way they can feel good about.

What if we, as a society, could step into the light and share the stories that burden us? Or, if we have been victorious in passing through the snares of trial and misfortune, why not share those lessons learned as a warning sign to others? What if we could open the door to a dialogue of healing and support? What if we could all stop believing we are the ONLY ONES DEALING WITH THIS? Our stories are all unique, but there is infinite crossover in the themes. To think we are the only one suffering is pretty selfish. Have we all become so callous that we refuse to carry the burdens of others? Sometimes I think so, but then I head to a comedy show and my hope is renewed.

When I have been in my darkest moments and endure struggles, I am careful to keep myself in check and private enough that people aren't worried about me all the time. Also, I simply detest complaining and feel it accomplishes nothing. My deep understanding for struggle and heartache helps me to be more compassionate toward others.

So, here we are. My life has turned to performance. I'm a comedian, or, as I like to call it, an inspirational humorist. Many people assume that I chose this vocation because I'm always HAPPY, but it is because of comedy that I can find relief from the things that trouble me. Comedy is my outlet. It helps me heal. It's because of the chaos and grief I've gone through/continue to go through that I do comedy. It's there when I'm angry or happy or sad. It's there when I feel like a crappy mother. It was the final thread to cling to when my postpartum depression spanned 11 stages of pure hell. It's there when my germophobia is in high gear, even though the microphone itself is a breeding ground for 60 million bacteria. It's even there when my road rage makes me want to activate a live-action bumper car game. It's there when my marriage hits the skids, and then when my marriage hits the skids, and again, when my marriage hits even more skids.

Comedy has been a lifesaver for me many times, and I've seen how vital it is for everyone around me. Making people laugh helps them leave their fears and cares behind, temporarily, and be okay with who they are in that instant. Having the ability to make people laugh is a responsibility I take very seriously. So seriously that I tattooed "Serious About Comedy" on my back. Don't judge me.

CHAPTER 2
Little Shop of Horrors

I was the girl who took the more difficult classes (like chemistry, YUCK) during summer school to pave the way for a carefree, fun-filled school year. I needed room in my schedule for two choir classes senior year. I had priorities! A cappella was second period and filled with lots of friends and plenty of goofing around because the class was so big. Capital Singers, though, was elite status, and I put on my game face in there, wrapping up the day strong in sixth period. I wasn't very good at reading music so I had to pay close attention to listen and learn my alto parts, mostly by ear. I was fairly sure the only reason I'd gotten into Singers was because two of my older siblings had been in it ahead of me. So, I certainly didn't take it for granted and I constantly made sure to work hard and prove my contribution to the ensemble was worthwhile.

I always wanted the solos, but never pulled off anything for the big competitions beyond a short scat solo during a jazz number called "Your Red Wagon." Scatting was a good fit for me to bop around blurting out sharp consonant sounds, and "dweedle-dah-bleeedop" my way through a solo instead of using boring ol' words. At least that's what I told myself.

Auditions came in late fall for the spring musical. I had my sights set on the role of Audrey in *Little Shop of Horrors*. I probably would have gotten it, too, if it hadn't been for that pesky Rachel Hitchcock, with all of her poise and professional singing lessons, experience in theater since she was a young child, and dripping with raw, natural talent. People often said we were twins, but only in regards to our long blonde hair and bubbly personalities. Things worked out for the best, since I really only wanted to sing the songs and had no interest in memorizing a ton of lines and queues anyway. I'm much better at making things up on the fly and apparently scatting wasn't appropriate for this production.

I was cast as a doo-wop girl along with a batch of my gal pals. I had only one line as a solo but plenty of other musical moments throughout the show, three whole wardrobe changes, and a bouffant hairdo that added oodles of volume and four inches to my short, thin frame.

My boyfriend, Brent, was always there. He was the drummer for both choirs, along with the musical production as well. Calm down, ladies. We hung out a lot initially out of general coincidence, but, before the fall had phased to winter, we were an item.

We spent more time together outside of school activities than we should have, but he was an upbeat fella and he always showered me with compliments, so keeping him around was good for my budding ego.

My parents didn't have very strict rules for me regarding curfews, and I didn't elaborate much into detailing which evenings I was at work or just hanging out with friends. They trusted me, and to be fair, 80 percent of the time I could be trusted 100 percent of the time.

I was the kind of daughter anyone would be proud of. An all-star young lady. Here I was, this spunky, high-energy choir nerd. I was in just about every "club" available, student council, and even rode the bench like a champ in basketball sophomore year. All the while I maintained a high level of activity at church as well and was the class president of my youth group several years in a row. I was the poster child of *happy and hardworking* with a bright future.

I wore very little make-up and modest, simple clothes, most of which I bought myself. Nothing too wild, although I loved getting old camouflage fatigues from the thrift shops, and kept a few other gems in regular rotation, like the screen-printed t-shirts that read "I Am the Woman from Nantucket," and "It Took Me 40 Years to Look This Good." My thick, long, wavy golden locks flowed all the way down to my waist and had never been dyed or cut into wild hairstyles and, in fact, were commonly pulled back in sets of two. Two braids, two buns, two ponytails. I had straight teeth without the help of braces. My grades were solid and I was very responsible. I started working my first official job the day after I turned 15, creating ice cream treats at the Dairy Queen down the street from where I lived.

As the youngest in a family with six children, we were taught to work hard and earn money (not just handed an allowance) to pay for our extracurricular activities. I paid my own way through driver's training as soon as I was old enough, so I could gain access to "The Deluxe," a 1979 Toyota Corolla Deluxe Edition. Rollin' up to school in that light brown tin can was good enough for me. I knew how to handle it like a pro, pulling cookies in the parking lot at just the right speed and angle, that when I hit a speed bump it launched the whole hunk of junk high enough to catch some sweet air before crash-landing directly on top of parking curbs, high-centered. I timed it conveniently nearby the football practice that was just ending so I called a few guys over to lift the car back to ground level.

At the launch of my senior year, I swapped over to a new job at "TCBY," a frozen yogurt shop where I quickly earned supervisory roles.

Where was I going with this? Oh yeah, I'm responsible!

It just so happened that I kind of sometimes took advantage of the good-kid persona I'd worked so hard to build. Sometimes I pushed the limits intentionally, other times it was just coincidence. I never lied when questioned, but when left to my own devices, I'd simply avoid offering additional information.

At least a few times a week after rehearsals for *Little Shop*, Brent and I would head to his house. We played a lot of video games and ate junk food. Sometimes we'd play with the drum set in the basement. Normal youth stuff. His parents would return home like clockwork, so we always knew exactly how much alone time there would be, although I'm not certain if either of us spoke of that observation out loud.

We'd been going steady for a whole three months or so at the time and so we pretty much had life figured out.

One afternoon, much like every other leading up to that point, there was a shift in the mood. I don't remember consciously deciding that would be the day I would let my guard down with him, but I also hadn't chiseled a firm plan for "no" or "we can't do this" well ahead of time like we are taught in church and in anti-drug rallies at school once a year. Plus, the thought occurred to me, that day I was wearing a particular new bra. I was a teenager and really had no good reason for owning a leopard-print bra, but I had it, and I felt different about myself in that moment. Like I'd already stepped into the danger zone, because even wearing something like that makes you want to show someone. It was the first thing I'd ever purchased from Victoria's Secret, which, for me, was a completely different ball game. Up until then my unmentionables were always from places like Fred Meyer's or Mervyn's.

Needless to say, one thing led to another and before I knew it, things happened, and my mind was yelling, "Oh, crap!" But it was too late. Reaction time has to be lightning-quick when you are young fumbling teenagers because things happen exceptionally fast. (Nothing personal, Brent.)

That moment hit my conscience like a freight train.

When it was over, I felt numb. Just that quickly I snapped into a brand new reality. Our relationship took a sharp turn into seriousness.

I excused myself, collected my things, and darted across the room to the nearest bathroom. I sat in there for what felt like hours. There was an eerie calm that swept over me. I hadn't ever had very detailed lessons on the birds and the bees, but I wasn't as naïve as I liked to pretend I was. All that hype society likes to build up about sex and I just kept thinking, "That was it?" (Again, nothing personal to Brent.)

Then, suddenly, the thought crept in that I could have just created a new life, mere moments ago. I couldn't shake it. I looked at myself in the mirror, and the girl staring back at me was completely stoic. The house was so quiet in that moment I swear I could hear the blood rushing through my own veins. I blinked a few times to try and clear the reflection. I felt a strong sense of true responsibility take over. I remember standing up a little straighter for a moment. Taking a few deep breaths. I tilted my head as I continued to gaze at that girl across from me. It was like I knew what was coming and for the quickest moment I wasn't afraid.

Then I heard his older sister come barreling down the stairs, announcing her arrival. I snapped out of my trance, flushed the toilet, and splashed a little water on my rosy cheeks before I mustered up the confidence to open the door. She eyed me curiously as I emerged. As far as I know, Brent and I played it cool, and we were in the clear, for now.

The days and weeks that followed were a blur. I maintained my usual schedule of school, rehearsals, and work, all the while feeling like I was a different person. Inadvertently, I had advanced my maturity level by 10 years. It was like this incessant white noise all around me. I'd listen to the conversations people would have in school and suddenly everything seemed so miniscule and inconsequential. Didn't anyone have any REAL problems?

Luckily, I hadn't gotten the starring role in the play because I could care less about a pretend world on a stage. I had a very real-life concern looming in my mind and I couldn't think of anything else.

I felt like I already knew I was pregnant, but I didn't dare admit it to myself. Before I knew for sure, just to be safe, I consciously sucked my stomach in. From the moment I woke, until I fell asleep again at night. All day. Every single day. It was the only logical thing I could think of doing under the circumstances. I starved myself because I didn't want to gain too much weight. I ate a little breakfast some days, but rarely any full meals. Primarily, I ate frozen yogurt. A tiny cup here, a sample cup there. Never much, but just enough to taste the flavors and feel the coldness melting down my throat. During quiet moments alone in the frozen yogurt shop, I'd savor the sweet taste of White Chocolate Mousse and wonder if I'd ever taste it again when I felt happy.

The more that thought did laps around my brain, the more worried I became. I tried to keep calm and feign positivity, like Brent was. He always had a cheesy grin plastered on his face.

Is there anything more aggravating than dealing with a sticky situation and having someone try so hard to be that optimistic silver-lining person? Already looking at the bright side when you are trudging through the muck and mire of a situation? Brent was that guy. He wanted to add a happy, smiling, "it's-going-to-be-okay" element to my day and I just wanted to throat check him half the time.

It didn't take long for a full month to elapse, and then another. I privately tried to convince myself that the first month that I missed my period was just a fluke thing. It was because of all the stress. Even after the third month lapsed, I still held onto a twinkle of hope for a miracle. Surely God wasn't going to let me carry this burden. Not me, not now. It was all so unreal.

I slipped quickly into a steady mode of denial where I remained for months to come. My world was unraveling around me, but I did my best to hold it together. Careful strategizing helped me determine my cover story and it was simple, I'd just never open my mouth to tell a single soul besides Brent. He didn't like the idea of keeping this a secret, but he reluctantly abided, and maintained his efforts to cheer me up.

I couldn't stand his upbeat attitude, and I resented him every time he talked about plans with friends after school or on the weekends. I had no interest in hanging out with people. Spending time with people I knew would make it impossible to go covert until the storm blew over.

With springtime came the bustle of choir performances, including the "Singers Show" – something I'd dreamed of being a part of since my older brother's Singers Show in 1994. Brent and I auditioned for a duet, Celine Dion's "Power of Love." We hammed it up a little too much, and it didn't exactly move people, except maybe to shift uncomfortably in their seats. Mrs. Schmidt, my teacher, looked at us like she hoped we were joking. Brent really wanted to perform that song together, but I felt like it was a terrible idea. I went along with it because he was so excited about it—it was to be the crown jewel of our high school careers.

In her wisdom, Mrs. Schmidt pulled me aside and asked me to select a solo piece for the concert. She expressed that she wanted my performance to be a moment where I could shine on my own.

It took me a while to make my selection, but I found the perfect fit.

Early May 1999, the show began and the energy in the auditorium was extraordinary. I absorbed the evening and tried to appreciate it for what it was and attempted to set aside my concerns. I was getting over a terrible cold and was filled with anxiety about my performance. I really wanted to nail the song, and leave my mark.

When it was my turn, I stepped out onto the stage. The spotlight poured over me. I sang "Angel" by Sarah McLachlan. Each word carefully spilled out, as I remained cautiously clenched in effort to prevent a coughing fit, or a flood of tears.

My eldest sister, Erin, recalls thinking it was strangely intense, noting that I barely held it together. By the end of the night, I was back to the forced smiles and everyone moved forward, none the wiser.

I was grateful when the school year finally came to a close.

As I sat in the large pavilion for the graduation ceremony, I was a bit somber that my memories of departure from "the best days of my life" were tarnished with a heavy reality. I felt some comfort in knowing that I was ultimately part of this giant blur of people being sent out into the world. My class numbered about 550 students. I listened as each name was called. There were many names I had never heard before, and likely would never hear again. I hoped that was the case for many people in that room when they read my name aloud. Walking across the stage, with an audience of six or seven thousand people, I maintained an intentional focus to avoid waddling, or heaven forbid, tripping and falling off the stage. I've never been so paranoid in all my life, with all eyes on me for that brief moment. They saw me, yet they saw nothing at all.

My MOTHER, ANN'S, STORY

I believe that everything happens for a reason. At least, in my life, that usually seems to be the case. I think there was a reason that I went nine months not knowing that my teenage daughter was pregnant, even though she was living right under my nose. I think I probably would have been pretty distraught and my two cents worth of advice maybe wouldn't have been what she would have needed through this experience. Part of me wishes I could have been there for her at this very difficult time in her life, and another part of me thinks I might not have been able to help her make the best decision for the future of her baby. I really had no experience with unplanned pregnancies. It also never occurred to me that she could even get pregnant. Not that I had talked to her about sex—I guess I thought that subject had been covered at church.

I don't remember a lot about that time because I wasn't aware of what was going on with Megan. My recollections are only snippets. In April of 1999, Brad and I were chaperones on a high school choir trip to Victoria, British Columbia. We went because we wanted to do something memorable with Megan, who was our baby, and who would be graduating from high school soon. The trip was right after the shootings at Columbine High School and it seemed like the news coverage of the tragedy was the only thing on TV in the hotel where we were staying. We expected it would be a fun time to spend with her, but she seemed distant. Was it because of the news coverage? She looked tired all the time and slept at the back of the bus a lot. She seemed disconnected and not her usual happy and fun-loving self. We thought she simply wasn't feeling well.

In May we went shopping for a prom dress. I remember helping her in the dressing room and wondering why she was gaining so much weight. She would have been about five months along. For some reason Brent was there, too. I thought that was kind of weird, but still I didn't jump to any conclusions. They must have wondered if I had fallen on my head or something not even to question why she was getting so heavy. I remember trying to pull up her zipper and thinking that her boobs were getting huge.

She worked a lot that summer. She has always been a hard worker, so for her to be working two jobs didn't seem strange to us. One was at the DoubleTree Inn doing catering and the other was at TCBY decorating cakes. She had graduated from high school and was just doing her own thing. I remember driving her to work at DoubleTree for some reason; she was wearing a very blousy white shirt. It looked kind of like a men's large, white, dress shirt. I just thought it was what she was supposed to wear to work. A big, comfortable work uniform.

That September, Brad and I went on our annual trip to the Oregon Coast. We had just lost my dad in June, so decided to take my mother with us that year. When we arrived home, Megan's sister, Shannon, told us that Megan had just had a baby and that she was in the hospital. We rushed over to find her and saw that she wasn't alone. With her were two people I can't remember, and her oldest sister, Erin, who was there volunteering to take the baby. Erin had just had our second grandchild seven months earlier. We decided then and there, I think, that it probably wasn't in the best interest of the baby to keep her in the family like that. Looking back, I realize I should have stayed with Megan, but I had the feeling at the time that everything was being taken care of as best as possible and there wasn't much else I could do. I didn't feel like it was my place all of a sudden to say, "WHAT HAVE YOU DONE! I'm taking over the situation now."

Brent stayed with her in the hospital that night.

Brad and I met with Brent's parents the next day to talk. We discussed all the ins and outs and pros and cons to the situation. We came to the conclusion, at least Brad and I did, that it was probably not a good idea to have them marry and keep the baby. Brent was a senior in high school at the time.

A few days later, we were at the Social Services office. We spent a little time with Megan and the baby. The baby had spent the few nights between the hospital and the adoption day in the home of a lady who takes care of babies waiting to be placed for adoption. Then we met the baby's new parents and older sister. They seemed very nice. After the two families met, laughed and cried—both sad and happy tears—Hannah and her new family left to go home.

CHAPTER 3
Into Hiding

When I was 16 years old, I got second piercings in both of my ears. I also got the cartilage of the top of my left ear pierced. I went home and my mother immediately informed me that I will be taking those piercings out. She calmly but firmly stated, "You look like a barbarian." I was ticked. A barbarian?!? Please. I looked cool. Super cool. The coolest I've ever looked! I was determined to keep my second holes pierced, but reluctantly agreed to taking out the one in the cartilage the same day I got it.

I begrudgingly removed the stud from my ear while I lay in a grumpy lump on my bed. A little stuffed angel hung from the switch on the swing-arm reading lamp on my wall overhead. My eyes were filled with tears, mostly because it hurt way worse than I thought it would, but also because I was embarrassed. And angry that something that seemed so trivial to me was being made into such a big deal. I took that tiny cubic zirconia stud and stabbed it right through the puffy hand of that angel. Point proven!

Just a few years later, in October 2000, I ultimately removed the second piercings when a message from President Gordon B. Hinkley, the prophet of my church, was issued in the general

conference. Among many important and urgent topics directed at parents and youth, it was announced that young women
should only have one set of piercings with modest jewelry. I was
happy to oblige the simple request. Those second holes were
constantly infected anyway, and still get infected to this day,
almost two decades later.

I recognized at that time that many of the matters that plague
our society range from seemingly trivial, like a second set of
earrings, to very damaging and addictive habits including drugs,
alcohol, and pornography. Not all of our choices can be seen by
everyone around us. Many choices and addictions can lurk as a
quiet, persistent demon behind closed doors.

We are taught as members of the Church of Jesus Christ of
Latter-day Saints (LDS,) as in many other Christian-based re-
ligions, to "abstain from all appearance of evil," (Thessalonians
5:22) and I think that sometimes people are guilty of becoming
so preoccupied with how they appear on the outside that they
lose focus and effort on actually living the life they are trying so
hard to portray. It is a slippery slope of lies and deception.

Honesty. What a crisp, delicious word. I love it. Say it out
loud. Especially if you are in a room with other people or on a
plane. Yell it! Listen to how clean and clear it is? Even if you just
whisper it (go ahead), its consonant sounds slice through the air
with purpose.

I want to live in honesty-ville, where I'm the mayor. The best
thing about honesty? It's always accurate. You don't have to remember what you said or to whom. It helps keeps your conscience free from the burden of juggling an alternate reality.
How quickly a web is woven with just a little fib.

Yeah, this is coming from a gal who hid her pregnancy, which
is all the more reason to trust me.

Let's back up here for a minute as I expand upon why hiding
an entire pregnancy is absolutely ludicrous for me. Perhaps it

is because I share the birthday of February 22nd with George Washington, albeit 249 years later, that I cannot tell a lie. I physically struggle with fibbing. Any time I want to avoid telling a whole truth, or admitting to something, even as simple as keeping a secret about a surprise, I get shifty-eyed, shrug my shoulders in a lurching and awkward manner, and kinda shake my head with a rubber-faced look of consternation like I don't understand the question. Instead of uttering something I know is untrue, I physically buckle under pressure and either have to excuse myself or ultimately break down and spill the truth.

I first realized this was true when I was about eight or nine years old and riding in the back seat of my mother's car. She inquired about the occupation of one of my friend's mothers. I had no idea what she did for a living, yet I stammered and attempted to make something up that sounded logical. My mother politely said, "If you don't know the answer, you can be honest. Just say, 'I don't know.'"

"Oh! Right," I replied, totally embarrassed. How silly was it that I hadn't realized it wouldn't make me less of a person by not knowing everything and just saying, "I have no idea, I'll ask"? My mother probably didn't even care that much and was most likely making small talk as we were out running errands.

In that case I wasn't even trying to cover up any naughty behavior or fib about anything worthwhile, yet there I was, physically shaken and hot-faced with embarrassment, because I didn't know how to fabricate a believable untruth even if I wanted to. But also, I felt stupid that I hadn't already concluded that there was no need to lie, ever.

After that, I never lied again. In rare cases where I didn't want to be COMPLETELY honest, I opted just to keep my yapper shut. When I open my mouth, honesty comes out. These days, that is a little more than people probably bargain for, but I can't stand lies and I won't contribute to the circulation of lies. I hate lying and playing games so much that blunt truth directed at my superiors has gotten me fired from my two highest paying jobs. I'll take ethics, a good-night's sleep, and unemployment over playing games with people, who have poor judgment and low standards, any day of the week.

So, to any of you out there who see me tight-lipped about something, now you know my secret.

I've always felt that telling the truth should be a safe and wonderful thing to do. Not enough people are completely comfortable with truth, because it is not always the easiest story to tell, and there is often that looming fear of what other people will think. (You know what I mean...people casting judgment on others to make themselves feel better. It's the worst! We'll talk about that later, but for now let's stay on the honesty train here for a bit longer.)

Still, I never, in a bazillion years would have expected that a time when I bravely, though reluctantly, shared my truth with two of my best friends that I would be made to feel so terrible. It was as if an immediate sentence of judgment was cast without hearing the full story. Just the thought lurking in my mind that I had had sex was overwhelming for me. It was scary, it was irreversible and finite. I was a changed person, and I truly felt like that was a change for the worse. How was I going to find a good, wholesome man to marry me someday? I was damaged goods.

But, there was hope. Right? Of course there was! I had been raised in a church that taught about redemption and forgiveness. Everything was going to be okay! I needed help, but I didn't know how to get started.

One afternoon, I was riding home from school with my best friends. I was in the back seat alone, while they were in front, as driver and shotgun. I suddenly felt the urge to open up to them. I didn't know what I was going to say, but my heart was pounding and I didn't want to miss this moment.

A simple drive we had taken hundreds of times together on the street that connects our neighborhoods to the high school, just a half mile away, was about to change forever. There was no stopping me now. In as few words as possible I informed them about what had happened just several days earlier. Before I even finished getting the words out of my mouth, one of them started screeching at me. The tone of her voice is a little caustic by nature, but with anger and disdain behind it, it sounded even more demeaning, and I absorbed every word.

After what felt like an hour (likely only a minute or two), her eruption subsided, and we pulled up to the house in silence. Her words were ringing in my head, and, all at once, I felt like this awful, worthless person, and I thought that she was right; everything she had said must be right.

How could I have been *SO STUPID*? What was I *thinking*? Everything was *ruined*, and I can't turn back time to take it back.

I was an idiot. I forfeited my standards. I was a lost cause.

As quickly as I had put the subject matter on the table, it was swept off and pushed into the past. I wouldn't dare bring it up again. There was no help to be had, and if that was the response from someone I believed to be among my very best friends, then surely I'd get the same reactions from other friends and loved ones. I couldn't bear the thought of unleashing that level of disappointment from the people I cared about most.

I became a quiet observer at school. I tried to envision what words I might select if I were going to tell someone what was going on. I looked at my friends and peers in the halls at school. I wondered what they would think about it, or if they would even care. Why would they? Heck, a lot of my peers had been having sex for years, so my story wouldn't have been all that shocking.

I did my best to avoid attention. I attempted to do well in my classes, while skulking around from time to time, angry at myself for throwing a wrench into my victory lap of high school.

The weeks passed. As more and more time elapsed and I didn't have the sweet relief of menses, I remained closed off.

The days kept rolling by. People just treated me like the Megan I'd always been. But I wasn't that girl anymore. It was somewhat shocking to me that people couldn't sense that something was going on. I had this secret that seemed as though it would manifest itself just by the general nature of pregnancies.

Spring came quickly. Brent and I both interviewed at the newest hot spot for teen apparel in the Boise Towne Square Mall. I was desperately clinging to the false reality that I could go on with life as usual. I was hired to work at the Buckle with the launch crew, and we opened the new store in March 1999. I jumped right into the experience with as much feigned enthusiasm as I could muster, focused on the goal of using my employee discount to get the most stylish Dr. Martens sandals on the shelves. The thought of those fat-stitched leather straps and two-inch-thick rubber soles slung to my narrow size six feet at the base of my gangly, unshaven legs became a welcomed distraction.

When I'd gone in for my interview, I kicked into typical Megan form. Bubbling over with smiles and adorable nerdiness. Admittedly, I wasn't expecting a job offer. I wasn't certain that I could fit in at this very fashionable clothing store. I was wearing a plain light yellow (not my color) ring-neck t-shirt from Old Navy, khaki cargo corduroys, and had two braids in my hair, Little-House-on-the-Prairie style, as I sat in a chair near the entryway of the store face to face with the hiring manager, Cid. I looked around me and observed all these attractive, hip teen applicants, but tried to tune them out and focus on being the most amplified Megan I could be. The conversation was fluid and flawless. It felt good to talk to someone I was meeting for the first time and have the comfort level to just be me. Throughout the interview, he was beaming and laughing at me. (Not with me.) But it was the good kind of laughing.

I was hired right away and helped launch the store for the grand opening. Fashion was not, and is still not, my strong point, and I remember thinking that this layering trend was going to take some *serious* getting used to. I felt completely out of place there. Cute skinny girls and their rich moms would wander into the store, and I was supposed to help them pick out their outfits? Um. No. I was the girl who managed to search out and purchase the least fashionable items in the entire shop. I couldn't picture myself in the cute trendy clothes, and I was drawn to the comfort zone afforded by the one style of cargo jeans in stock, this insane fuzzy yellow top with a Charlie Brown zigzag across the front, and, of course, the chunkiest clunky Dr. Martens sandals ever made.

I lasted six weeks there before I couldn't handle being a walking mannequin anymore. I wasn't exactly the model of fashion anyway, but certainly not with my poochy tummy. With a growing belly bump on the horizon, it was becoming a priority to remain inconspicuous. It was much too risky to work in a place where I was going to be looked at, my outfits judged, on a daily basis.

I remember when a few people, including my mother, commented on my weight gain and general change in attitude when I was pregnant. I would shrug my shoulders and purse my face with a look like "I dunno what you're talking about..." and move on to a new subject as soon as possible.

It was time to go covert with this operation. I was already working at a TCBY frozen yogurt shop at the time, and replaced the Buckle quickly with a job in the catering department at the DoubleTree Hotel in Garden City. My goal was simple: never be home where my family might catch on to my expanding stomach. I'd committed to doing everything possible to avoid the people who loved me the most, and confined myself into a strategy of isolation, even in plain sight.

CHAPTER 4
Planned Parenthood

Last summer we planted a garden. Well, more like a yarden, because our house sits on a very tiny lot, so the entire space of our little backyard was taken over by garden.

What an incredible experience it was. From packets of seeds, to fruits and vegetables that we could step right outside and harvest each day throughout the season.

I helped push the seeds into the little starter dirt pods. As I poured out the packet of watermelon seeds into my hand, I was astounded to think that tiny little black oblong fleck was going to sprout, a tiny bit each day, and become a heavy seven or eight-pound juicy melon. Can anyone deny that would happen, provided it was nurtured and cultivated with water and sunlight? I didn't doubt for a moment what the potential was of that little singular seed. Life, in every form, is mind-boggling to me, and I could feel all that potential sitting right on my sweaty palm.

We had a full variety of fruits, veggies, and flowers. One particular pot of flowers was growing too crowded and we thinned it out by plucking a few tender little stems that hadn't yet reached full bloom. In no way negating that they were still flowers, by divine nature, and in a constant, steady mode of growth around the clock.

In a few cases, a melon or cucumber was plucked from the vine too early by my two-year-old. These fruits hadn't been able to fully ripen and had a bitter taste. I thought to myself, "What a waste!" If only they hadn't been snapped from their stems prematurely.

Watching this garden grow and thrive was a deeply poignant experience for me. I quietly weaved around the plants every few days, examining their intricate details and running my fingers along the multitudes of textures. The prickly, hair-thin pines on the vines of the zucchini plant. The thick, braided ribbing of the corn husks, complimented by the wispy cluster of silk strands that pour out the top of each ear. The broad, hearty leaves of the pumpkin plants, stretched open like a net to absorb the sun rays, and siphon the morning dew down into its stem, funneling the delicate drops of water into the vine to feed the thirsty gourds.

The aroma of a growing garden is fresh and invigorating. Especially after a brief, heavy summer downpour. The plants wilt just slightly under the pressure, but quickly regain integrity and eagerly await the sunlight. Checking in at different times of the day, I observed the leaves steadily following the sun, diligently, instinctively, from east to west before closing up and resting for the night.

Growing a garden in my own backyard, spending time with my family working outside, and savoring the flavors of harvest, was inspiring. Life, in all capacities, will thrive unless it is interrupted, intentionally or otherwise. Even more encouraging, is that life can and will flourish on its own, because that is nature's way. This is a fact that you cannot simply deny.

Funny how much your mind can play games with you when you are terrified. Denial felt like the only safe place I could hide all those years ago. Yet, denial can only get you so far. During the season of growing a baby, there is a finite amount of time in play. Luckily, even though I couldn't see any light at the time, there was absolutely going to be an end to this tunnel.

There finally came a time when I had to stop denying to myself that I was pregnant. I felt the fluttering inside my belly. I could sense the life growing within. This little baby was a mover and a shaker, and had hiccups all the time. Flipping and flopping several times a day. She literally kicked me out of my denial.

YIKES. Now what?

I'd always been a very healthy kid and teen and didn't know what kind of doctor to seek out. I remember hearing about Planned Parenthood. I wasn't clear on exactly what their scope of work included, but the name *sounds* responsible. I needed to talk to people who were responsible, because I messed up and was in a crisis. (Please note: This is an account of *my personal* experience. I have to believe that many other people are completely satisfied with their services rendered or they would not still be in business.)

Planned – noun
A scheme or method of acting, doing, proceeding, making, etc., developed in advance.

Parenthood – noun
The state, position, or relationship of parent.

Planned Parenthood – noun (trademark)
A nonprofit organization that does research into and gives advice on contraception, family planning, and reproductive problems.

I'd heard it was affordable, and advertisements indicated I could find help there. So, I went to Planned Parenthood. Brent was with me, although his physical presence hardly warranted me giving him any direct attention. This was my problem, and he certainly couldn't comprehend what was going on in my mind. I was angry at him, but I was angrier at myself.

We walked into the clinic. I was greeted by a seemingly disinterested older gal and she handed me a few pages of paperwork on a clipboard to fill out. I reached over a bowl of condoms to take it from her. Too late for those. I could tell this was a pretty standard routine, and I'd become another number. Blending in felt okay in the moment, and I was glad my arrival hadn't been received with complete shock. I was just another screw-up kid here.

I took a seat, clicked the pen and made quick work of filling out the boxes. It was a sunny day, with rays of light pouring through the slats of the blinds as the dust particles shimmered. I felt calm. I was about to get help from people who understood what I was going through.

Before long I was summoned to the doorway that separated the gray quiet lobby from the beige colored hallway, bright with fluorescent lights. I made my way through what appeared to be cubicles made from tempered glass to get past the front desk, and over to the lab coat-wearing woman waiting for me.

She escorted me to the restroom and handed me a little cup for a urine sample to run a simple pregnancy test. I hadn't taken one of those yet.

Then we were off to the exam room. The woman didn't keep us waiting long.

There were two employees in the room with us. The monitor for the ultrasound machine was facing away from me, the volume off. One of them asked what type of prenatal care I'd been receiving up to that point, as she prepped my belly with a generous squirt of light blue jelly. I sheepishly replied that I had not gone into a doctor; that only Brent knew I was pregnant, and not a single other soul had been told. She gave me a look that made me feel like a moron.

"Well, you are definitely pregnant!" she exclaimed, still swirling the wand along my skin. After just a few moments, and several rapid clicks on the ultrasound machine, capturing pictures and measurements, it was over.

The women didn't say a whole lot, and excused themselves just briefly. Upon their return, I was immediately told that I was "a little too far along for what they would normally allow for a termination."

Termination? That didn't sound good. I sat and listened as she explained the process of removal, as if the baby wouldn't feel a thing. As if the baby was a THING. Not a living being. My heart broke.

I hadn't even considered abortion. I was so naïve, I hadn't even really thought about what it meant. And, I certainly couldn't fathom that process taking place after limbs, functioning organs, and a heartbeat were present. Does a growing baby fall under their description of a "reproductive problem?"

All I wanted was help. For someone to see me for the terrified young woman I was. I wanted someone to hold my hand and tell me everything was going to be okay. I quickly learned that this was not the place for that kind of reassurance. The woman quietly, but firmly, said she was sorry she couldn't help me.

There wasn't anything else they could do for me. I was too far along to abort. I was not offered any additional information about prenatal services for the duration of the pregnancy. That was not in their wheelhouse of services, apparently. I was 18 years old, but still on my parent's insurance. They suggested I tell my parents, but I already decided that was not an option.

There was no suggestion about looking into adoption, nor anything as simple as a pamphlet on the subject. No resources provided to me.

A little overwhelmed and confused, I was shown the way back to the lobby. I wasn't sure what to say or ask for. I felt like a stupid kid who made a stupid mistake, and it wasn't their duty to help me.

I felt more hopeless than ever. I was being ushered out without any offer of prenatal information, and the option of adoption was never explained. I wrote a check that nearly drained my high-schooler's bank account for the services rendered, though I'm not exactly sure WHAT services were rendered. They did nothing to help me.

I marked it in my check register as "Planned Party Hats" just in case anyone happened upon my financials. That was the best cover name I could think of? Ridiculous. Another example, I'm no good at fibbing.

I walked out the door of Planned Parenthood. The sun was still shining. The world was still turning. A few strands of my long blonde hair wafted across my face in the spring breeze. I inhaled deeply, and, with the exhale, determined that I had no other option but to charge forward, facing the predicament I'd gotten myself into without burdening anyone else. I was going to handle it on my own. Somehow.

CHAPTER 5
Nothing to See Here

I'm a people pleaser. It is a weakness of mine. This all stems from my childhood. I've been the center of attention as long as I can remember, and it always felt like people wanted me around. I was always the goofy one cracking jokes, talking in funny voices, singing songs, and other generally rambunctious behaviors. I was the one who could make people laugh.

I'm the youngest of six kids in a blended family, so naturally I'm a little attention hungry.

But, thinking back, there wasn't anything particularly noteworthy that happened in my home. Just a normal gaggle of kids brought together by a second marriage.

There were shared bedrooms, and even fewer shared bathrooms. When I was eight, there was a stint of time when my sister, Shannon, and I slept on the pull-out bed in the living room couch. I thought that was pretty cool because my mom and step-dad, Brad, were up late each night watching Carson or Letterman on the other side of the room, and I would listen in and try to figure out why they were laughing, since I didn't get many of the jokes at the time. Just hearing them chuckle was a great comfort, and I enjoyed the flickering blue light in the room as I drifted off for the night.

I always felt like we had a lot, because our house was full of people and stuff. I assumed hand-me-downs were standard in all households with a lot of kids, and thought it was a pretty slick deal when my older sisters and I would get matching outfits from my grandmother that I could maintain that style for years to come. For several years I alternated these outfits as I grew into them as my wardrobe selection for picture day at school. Red dress with a rainbow heart necklace in first grade, then a two-toned blue sweat suit the next year in second grade. By third grade I'd grown into my sister's red dress, and in fourth grade, you guessed it, I was back into the blue sweat suit another size up.

My biological father left when I was very young. He was pretty much MIA since day one for me, but officially left when I was three. He didn't bring my mother and me home from the hospital after I was born. He was always busy working. He "never was a family man," according to his quote in a local newspaper when he was interviewed out at the race tracks where he frequently put the pedal to the metal in his navy blue Camaro. My mom logged the details of his whereabouts in my baby books, which I finally looked through in detail about a year ago. My first several birthdays indicated that he wasn't there at all, or that he was just in time for cake, but then out the door again to work.

Although my mother took these notes, diligently recording for posterity's sake, I don't recall a single time she spoke ill of him. I realized, as I reached adulthood, how truly remarkable that was, and what a wonderful woman she is all the way to her very core. She allowed me (and I assume my older siblings) to form our own opinions on the matter, and love him for who he was. He was my dad, but he wasn't my *dad*.

I don't have memories of him living at home. My earliest memories of my father are in the form of visits once or twice a year. He would take the four of us to the same restaurants on many of those visits; The Pantry for breakfast, Flying Pie Pizzeria for dinner, and we would play in the yard or go to a park to kill time feeding the ducks, tossing around an Aerobie, or attempting to fish in the river.

I enjoyed his visits very much, but I also enjoyed hanging out with Brad. I was young enough when my mother remarried that I wasn't jaded by the divorce like some of the older kids may have been. I was thrilled to have a father figure in the home full time and I built, and still maintain, a solid relationship with my step-dad. I like to think I'm his favorite, but I always like to think I'm everyone's favorite.

My life felt normal as I grew up. I loved the kind of attention I got when I was the one orchestrating it. I was either in performance mode, or I was in live-my-life-like-a-normal-respectable-person mode. I could control which mode I was in, and I liked that.

When my world began rocking due to this unplanned pregnancy, I was forced to deal with something that was totally out of my control. Some would argue that it was all within my control. I made a poor decision with my boyfriend that ultimately led to pregnancy out of wedlock. I hoped I could try to control the situation, but I knew it was beyond me. I knew there was a grand purpose to this life growing inside me, and my biggest fear was making the wrong decision for this baby. A close second was the fear of how this could negatively impact my friends and family.

As best as I could, I clung to living as normally as possible. Embracing the daily drill of working hard and being a good person. I didn't want anything to catch attention in a negative way. My steady, good reputation kept me off the radar. If at all possible, I would maintain that even-keeled, adequate amount of attention. Everything is fine, nothing to see here!

Even when I knew darn good and well that I was facing a nearly impossible feat of *hiding a pregnancy*, I remained committed to keeping up that outward appearance that all was well. But that proved to be physically and mentally exhausting.

I went prom dress shopping with my mother when I was just about five months pregnant. We slung several options over our arms and headed into the dressing room together while Brent loitered between clothing racks nearby. My belly had only begun to expand slightly by then, but my chest had grown substantially and she tried to gingerly broach the subject as she jostled me around, determined to get my body zipped into the next dress. "Your boobs are huge, Megan!" she blurted. She failed to keep it gingerly.

As quickly as possible, I selected a pale pink dress with a shimmery silvery-pink swirling pattern throughout the fabric. It looked and felt a little like fancy upholstery, and that was just what I needed. Something that wouldn't feel too clingy. I wore my hair up, and kept my accessories simple with white gloves and an artificial smile.

I didn't want to go to prom. I didn't want to do anything that involved me being around people, but I didn't want to let anyone down by being a party pooper. I felt at times that I owed it to Brent to check these events off the list so that he didn't miss out on important high school memories, too.

Miraculously, high school ended and it became much easier to disconnect from friends and maintain my busy and responsible work schedule.

When I took on the second job at the hotel, I had a new normal for the time being, and I held on tightly all summer.

At 5 a.m. the alarm went off. Another morning waking up in the seemingly endless nightmare of being awake. I sluggishly rubbed my eyes and hoisted myself off the top bunk while my older sister, whom I shared a room with, still slept. I reached

through the darkness to grab the half-empty bottle of Bath &
Body Works Coconut Lime Verbena Lotion from the top of my
dresser and slather a generous glop onto my elbows and my belly. Barely 18 and I remember wondering why my elbows were
always so dry and crusty.

I slapped on my ill-fitting uniform. I had men's slacks, a
frumpy white button-up, and a standard- issue DoubleTree Hotel vest. The integrity of my bra was declining. Gone were the
days of a single-closure brassiere.

I was out of the house by 5:15 to report for duty at 5:30. I was
always early for work. I liked to tell myself it was because I'm
an overachiever, but it was really because I needed to be out of
sight before anyone woke up in my home.

I'd often grab my breakfast to go, if I'd grabbed anything at
all. It was a 10-minute drive to work. Just the right amount of
time to consume the typical selection of "mobile cereal." There
was something oddly satisfying about drinking soggy Frosted
Mini-Wheats out of a Maverick mug. I knew just the right angle to get some cereal and a little milk without the whole thing
slopping onto my face and into my lap.

As I deduced in the dressing room with my mother, one of
the reasons the focus wasn't directly on my growing belly at the
time was because of my recent chest expansion. Later it was
confirmed that it just appeared that I was gaining some weight,
because I was packing on some puffiness in my face, breasts, and
stomach. Large bosoms have always been a package deal for the
duration of my pregnancies.

I didn't think much of it at the time, although I did have to go
up a size in my work uniform at the hotel. There was no denying
they were there, and I hated when it attracted unwanted attention. One of my co-workers in the banquet department, Bill,
who looked like a displaced mid-30s surfer dude from So Cal,
said "I'll do some of your work if you show me your boobs."

"HOW SWEET OF YOU!" I barked at him, with thick sarcasm. (I did not take him up on the offer, no matter how tired I got.)

Yuck. As if it wasn't bad enough that I was working myself to the bone, hauling mediocre breakfast entrees on giant trays stacked eight plates deep, or hoisting bins of "food" (i.e. slimy raw meats or produce that was on the brink of rotting) in and out of the walk-in refrigerators for prep with the chefs. Oh, wow, the smell of that walk-in fridge. It was like the show, "Kitchen Nightmares" before there was a show called, "Kitchen Nightmares." The last thing I needed was for some pig to make me feel like a piece of that slimy meat.

One particularly hot summer day, after I'd finished up my morning shift at the hotel, I had to swing by my house to pick up my dark green "TCBY" polo that I'd left in the dryer the night before. I ran inside to grab it, and then jumped back into the un-air-conditioned "Deluxe" and, as if it were a sporty Camaro, I pushed the (rusty) pedal to the metal (worn-out, ratty ol' floor board). It had crappy brakes and I had to drive down a decent sized hill near my house to get down the bench to the frozen yogurt shop.

In some of my darkest moments, I thought about how much easier life would be if I just jerked the wheel at the top of the hill near my house and took a tumble down the steep grade, or, if the light changed to red at just the right time, I could coast into the intersection just in time to be T-boned by a city bus as it innocently launched into its green light. While these were fleeting thoughts, looking back now, it is quite alarming to have been in that place of such despair that the very thought of death seemed like an easier way out.

When I finally made it to work, I went inside, uniform in hand, and headed straight for the walk-in freezer to change out of my sweaty white button-up shirt from the hotel. It felt good to be alone in a cold, refreshing, isolated space to catch my breath and cool my blazing red cheeks. I was surrounded by brightly colored cake boxes, crates of yogurt mix, and giant bags of Reese's Peanut Butter Cups. I would stare at these simple, inanimate objects with my eyes glazed over and ponder how incredible it was that I took the trivial things of day-to-day life for granted before. Nothing seemed simple now. Everything was overshadowed by a huge, unrelenting responsibility.

I made it a regular habit the rest of the hot summer days to carry in my work polo and spend a few moments cooling off in the dressing room/freezer, recalibrating before my shift started. I felt safe there. Just me and the frozen confections.

Occasionally, I had to fill shifts for "TCBY" during the open season for Roaring Springs, a local water park. I watched families splashing around, cooling off as the sun beat down. My little cart of frozen treats was perched on a cement slab next to the Lazy River. Oh, how I craved taking a lap around the park in the Lazy River, my tired heap of a self flumped over a signature blue float tube.

In July and August, Brad was building a big new workshop in our back yard for his business as an independent contractor. It wasn't uncommon for me to be out helping him, since I'd been on construction jobs with him since I was young. I didn't shy away from hard work. I don't remember exactly what I was doing some days, but there were nails and wood beams involved, while I stood sweating away at the top of an 18-foot structure prepping it for roofing. Don't feel bad for me. In general I actually liked that type of work. I learned how to lay tile by the time I was 10, and, if you needed demolition work, I could take down a room's worth of sheetrock with a crowbar in no time. It just might not have been the best idea to be doing that at eight months pregnant, but we've already established that sometimes I have lapses in good judgment.

Day by day, hour by hour, I trudged on. I kept a smile on my face, and I worked hard to be the best employee I could possibly be, so that any attention I was given was positive, and avoidant of my personal issue. I was focused on being as normal as possible, raising no flags that anything was askew in my life.

I graduated with a slew of Mormon guys who called themselves the "MoPo," short for Mormon Posse. One by one they started to head out to the far ends of the Earth to preach the Gospel. I attended more than a half-dozen mission farewells that summer. I wanted to be there to support my friends, and to leach off of the spirit of hope during their talks. I sat in the pews, in my baggiest dress, with my long hair draped over my shoulders. I hunched my back and recoiled my midsection with all my might, with hardly any breath left to breathe.

On a rare occasion, and usually with a lot of coaxing by Brent, I would come out of hiding in my usual busy schedule of hiding-ness to spend time with friends or family. One such occasion was for dinner at Mongolian BBQ with his family. His sister didn't like me. I could feel it in her eyes when she stared at me. I broke eye contact and focused on my bowl of noodles. I felt sick that day, like most days. I only ate a few bites because it was too hard to eat while sucking in my belly.

This wasn't my plan. This was not at all the way I pictured my summer going after finally being liberated from the dregs of high school life. But, it had been a plan with such perfectly orchestrated elements that I cannot deny that it was the plan of my Heavenly Father.

I'd say, all in all, I did an excellent job maintaining the normal behaviors of a busy, responsible teenager and carrying on with my life like it was business as usual on the outside. It wasn't until after the baby was born that people mentioned how much I had NOT been behaving like myself.

Apparently I was a distant, closed-off version of myself, and not at all the up-beat and genuinely happy person everyone knew and loved. But, since I hadn't let my guard down, there wasn't any reason for people to be too concerned. Either people chalked it up to me stretching myself too thin with work, or being stifled by a boyfriend, who many of my friends and family later noted was a little too clingy.

CHAPTER 6
Meanwhile, in Washington

When the parents who would someday adopt my first-born child got married, I was a spunky seven-year-old living in Idaho, just a mere state line away, and not a care in the entire world. Leanne, like many women who choose to adopt, struggled for years to get pregnant before ultimately choosing to look into adoption. It would be a wait, surpassing an entire decade in length, before she would be driving to Boise to pick up her second child.

I cannot fathom having to struggle with having babies. Sometimes I feel a little guilty with how easy it has been for me to have my children. Obviously, it happened when I wasn't even trying to get pregnant, or we wouldn't be here flipping through the pages of my life. When I was ready for a family of my own, I planned it out, and boom, pregnant. All three times since. Granted, it took me eight years to want to get pregnant because my first pregnancy was a living nightmare, but once I was ready to go, pow, a bun was in the oven.

I consider the emotional and physical battles women must endure if they have issues with infertility and resolve to turn to adoption, and my heart breaks even more knowing that their ability to experience the joy of parenthood is reliant on another woman making the decision to hand over their own baby.

When I think of everything that Leanne endured with infertility and her inability to conceive a child, the one thing she wanted more than anything else in this life, I realize how crucial it was for our paths to cross. I'm humbled by the role I was able to play in her life.

LEANNE'S STORY

Infertility. I used to hate that word. It meant the "inability to reproduce by natural means." It also came to mean so much more to me. It meant sadness and sometimes anger. It meant emptiness—not only my empty womb, but my empty, aching arms. It was brokenness—feeling that my body had betrayed me. Oftentimes, it was jealousy—the joyful pronouncements of pregnancies and baby showers were the worst. It was always longing—it was hard not to stare at other mothers with their babies. It was begging and pleading on my knees. Sometimes doubting—maybe I wasn't good enough. And tears; lots and lots of tears.

Infertility. I *used* to hate that word...

From the time I was a little girl, I dreamed of becoming a wife and stay-at-home mom.

In May of 1988, I became a bride and half of my dream joyously came true. I married a wonderful man, Wayne, who loved me very much. I knew the other half of my dream would quickly become a reality and I would begin my perfectly happy life. In my naive mind, I assumed that shortly after we were married, we would have the wonderful news to share that we were expecting.

A few months went by and hmm…I guess it takes a little longer than I thought. Six months came and went but I told myself not to panic. I had heard that it takes the average couple a year to get pregnant.

When a year turned into two, many of our friends were announcing their happy news. I would receive it with a smile on my face and an ache in my heart.

As two years turned into three, it started to become unbearable. What was wrong? Every single month was torture. My period was the enemy. The worst were those months when my cycle would be a few days late. My mind would be consumed all day with the glimmer of hope that maybe there were the beginnings of a tiny life forming inside of me. I obsessed over every little detail of my body, torturous thoughts all day long, "I think my breasts are a little more tender this month." "I swear I am urinating more often." "Was that a wave of nausea I just felt?" When these particular months would mock me, I would spend so much time on my knees. I would plead with God to please let this be the month. I begged Him to create a miracle for Wayne and me. I could picture in my mind that fertilized egg, that embryo. But to no avail. My period would come, *every time.*

Wayne was still in college so we couldn't afford any major fertility treatments. I had health insurance through my work, but it didn't cover infertility, which was typical. The hardest part was that no one could really explain what our problem was. The few tests we did have showed that I ovulated every month and my husband's sperm count was just fine. My body didn't destroy his sperm. My fallopian tubes were wide open. There was no medical reason why we weren't conceiving. We were diagnosed with unexplained infertility. That diagnosis was more depressing than if there really was something wrong. At least, then, we would have an answer and maybe a treatment plan going forward.

In March of 1995, Wayne was just shy of graduating from pharmacy school. I was getting very anxious for that time to come. I was hoping that he would find a job with insurance that provided some type of help for fertility treatments. I remember one day, in particular, when I was thinking about it and had an overwhelming feeling that we should look into adoption. I kind of shrugged it off because I really wanted to dig a little deeper into our infertility issues before we made a different decision. The more I tried to dismiss the thought about adoption, the more it persisted. I remember walking into the living room to talk to Wayne about the feelings I was having. I said "I think we are supposed to look into adoption," and then I burst out bawling. I wasn't crying because I felt defeated and this was something we were going to have to resort to, I actually was very humbled by the prospect of being chosen by someone to love and raise their child. At the end of the conversation, we decided we would start to look into adoption and see what it entailed and how we felt as we continued to move forward with that decision. I started to get really excited.

The next nine months were a blur of paperwork, interviews, and home visits, but also miracle after miracle as we walked through the doorway that was labeled, "adoption." When we got the news that we were approved, we were informed that the average wait for a baby was 18 months. Even though it seemed like a long time to wait, I felt comfort in knowing that we were waiting for something more concrete. This was different than another year and a half of broken hearts, month after month.

Three weeks after we were approved, we got a phone call that turned our world upside down. A young woman was pregnant and had chosen to place her baby for adoption. She wanted us to be her baby's parents. We were told that she was due in three weeks and that she would like us to write her a letter. That was the hardest letter I have ever written. How do you adequately express to someone you have never met, but is trusting you with her baby, just how deeply humbled and thankful you are? There are no words that can do justice to the feelings of the heart in a situation such as this. I realized her selfless act would bring us immense joy, but would cause her great pain. The thing I wanted most to do was to hug her long and hard and then to look her in the eyes and tell her how brave she was. I wanted to tell her that I knew I would never fully understand how hard this was for her. But most of all, I wanted to tell her we would love her baby with all of our hearts, and that her child would grow up always knowing of her and her sacrifice, and how much we love her for it.

For the next three weeks, all I could do was pace the floor and cry. So many thoughts ran through my head. How is she doing? What if she changes her mind? Is this really happening? And the prayers. Oh, the prayers.

Our phone rang on December 25th at 11 p.m. The voice on the other end told us that we had a beautiful baby girl with lots of hair, a Christmas miracle. She wanted us to know that her birth mother told the nurses to do everything they could to help the baby be born that day. She didn't want another Christmas to go by with us being childless. I was overcome with emotion. I was so amazed that, in her hours of pain and childbirth, she was still focused on us.

The next day, we drove five hours to get our daughter. We rode in silence as I was too consumed with emotion to speak.

When we arrived at the agency, it was after hours. We were met by our birth mother's social worker. I don't think my feet touched the floor as I rushed to the baby carrier that rested on the floor. Inside was the most angelic little round face I had ever seen. I immediately scooped her up into my arms. The bond I felt to this precious infant was immediate. I was finally a mother and there was no doubt that this baby was meant to be mine. Wayne and I stood, side by side, in awe as we studied this precious child. In that room, the influence of God was there. In that sacred moment, a family was created. We named her Katelyn Elizabeth.

We didn't stay at the agency for long. I wanted to go to our hotel and be together, just the three of us. When we walked into our room, I was surprised to see a very nice and plush recliner/rocking chair. I was able to sit all night and rock my sweet baby like I had always dreamed of doing. I had never been in a hotel room with a rocking chair and have never seen one since. God didn't even leave that detail out. As I rocked and snuggled with my tiny daughter, the tears would not stop flowing. I could not stop thinking about her birth mother. I prayed that, in her time of sorrow, she would be blessed with a great sense of peace. I prayed that she would know her baby was loved.

For the next two years, I cherished my time as a stay-at-home mother with my sweet daughter. My days were so full of laughter and learning and fun. Our little girl was smart and funny and talkative! At such a tiny age, she would strike up a conversation with people wherever we went. People would look at me astonished and ask how old she was. When I stated her age, they would look at her incredulously!

Katelyn's adoption required that we have correspondence once a year with her birth mother until she was five. We looked forward to that time every year. We loved not only giving her updates as to how well Katelyn was doing, but also getting to hear what was happening with her. We were ecstatic when we learned that she had gotten married and was expecting a baby. When the five-year mark came, it was really hard to have the correspondence end, but I was happy that she hoped that Katelyn would want to meet her after she turned 18. I looked forward to that day immensely.

Around the time that Katelyn turned two, we started to talk about submitting our paperwork in hopes of adopting another baby. The next six months were spent completing more forms, interviews, and home studies. We were, again, told the average wait was 18 months. This go around the time frame ended up being spot on.

Fourteen months into the waiting process, we got a call that a birth mother had chosen us. She was pregnant with a baby girl. She wasn't due for another three months, but she wanted to start corresponding with us in the time she had left. We happily agreed. We started writing letters back and forth but something just didn't sit quite right with me. I had a certain sense that this was not going to work out. True to my feelings, we got a call a couple months later letting us know that she had decided to parent her baby. I wasn't surprised. I cried for about half an hour and then I was okay. I felt that God had prepared me for this. I mostly cried for her and her little one. I hoped, with her being so young, that she and her baby would be okay.

Two months later on a Saturday morning, we were preparing to leave the house to travel to a city an hour away to do some shopping. The phone rang and it was our social worker on the other end. He asked me if Wayne was home and to get him on the other phone. Our social worker said, "I am standing on one leg trying to do my best stork impression because a baby girl was born three days ago, and the birth parents have chosen you to be her parents. You can come and get her on Monday." Just like that we had another daughter! It was exciting and scary all at once. Words cannot describe the feelings that run through your body when you get news like that. I felt like I would burst with happiness. He went on to explain that this was the quickest adoption in which he had ever been involved. He said that the birth mother hid her pregnancy the whole nine months. She lived with her parents and they didn't know. I was astounded! How was that even possible? He said that the only two people who shared this secret were the birth mother and birth father. I listened intently but in awe as he continued with the story. He said that her parents were away on a trip when she went into labor. She finally broke down and told her sister that she was not only pregnant but also in labor! Her sister drove her to the hospital where she delivered her baby. Her parents had to be called and told the news that their youngest daughter was not only in the hospital, but had delivered a baby girl, and they needed to come home. I was in shock over this story. How on earth do you keep this huge secret from the world? My heart went out to this family! I felt sorrow for the young couple who held such a huge weight upon their shoulders and carried it alone. I felt sadness for a mother who was just learning that her daughter had given her a grandbaby, a baby that she knew nothing about. As excited as I was about this baby, my heart held a lot of grief for this family.

The birth family requested a meeting with us and scheduled to meet us on Monday morning. On Sunday, we drove the same direction that we took almost four years before. Our daughters were born in the same town.

That Monday will always hold a special place in my heart. Meeting face to face with, not only the birth mother and her parents, but also the birth father and his parents, was such a precious and spiritual experience. It was amazing to meet the people who were willing to sacrifice their wants and desires for what they felt was best for this little life. It is so humbling to be the recipient of that sacrifice. I don't remember exactly the order that the meetings happened, but I remember talking to the birth father's parents. They seemed very supportive of the decision that was made. They were very kind and told us about their son, what he was like growing up as a child. They told us that he was a very caring person who thought of others first. They were very concerned that we had cats because their family had severe allergies and wanted to make sure that we kept a good eye on the baby for any reactions. We promised we would.

When we met with the birth mother's parents, I felt a little more on the cautious side. For some reason, I had really tender feelings for our birth mother's mother. I wanted her to feel at peace. I knew she was hurting for more than one reason, and I just prayed that she could feel good about us and know that we would take very good care of her grandbaby. I remember them telling us that their daughter was a very caring person. She was always concerned for other people. I was grateful that both of our baby's birth parents had caring personalities. That would come to make a lot of sense as our daughter grew.

Finally, we met with the birth couple, Megan and Brent. I was amazed by their maturity. They were fun-loving and upbeat. As I was anticipating this meeting, I pictured a bawl-fest, but it wasn't that way at all. They were very easy to talk to. They told us that they named the baby Emma Faye and wanted to know what we planned on naming her. We told them Hannah Nichole. They seemed happy with that. They said at least Hannah kind of rhymes with Emma. Sort of. I really enjoyed spending time with them. One thing, they said, stuck out to them as they read our profile. It was that we had a Jeep. I thought it was funny that, of all the things that could draw them to us, that was one of them. I was glad that God guided my hand when I wrote the letter 18 months earlier to potential birth parents, and that it included that little tidbit. They were excited for us to see the baby. They kept saying, "Wait until you see how beautiful she is." When our meeting came to an end, we hugged each other and said our goodbyes. It's hard sitting in front of the two people who are giving you this amazing gift, and then watch them walk away. I remember Megan turning in the hall to look at us one last time. She said that she wanted to burn us into her memory. Thinking about it even now makes me cry.

After meeting with all of the family, it was time to meet our new baby daughter for the first time. One of the social workers walked into the room carrying the baby. I was sitting in a chair and Wayne was standing beside me. They placed this tiny girl, dressed in a little pink sleeper, into my arms. She had very long fingers and a sweet little face. As I stared at her, studying her, I could feel all of the eyes on me in the room. I remember feeling awkward with all of the attention.

I don't recall Wayne taking her from me, but in the pictures taken at the agency, he was the one holding her. They brought our daughter Katelyn into the room to meet her baby sister. I remember her being happy and wanting to hold her right away. She wanted to name her Nellie because in the movie, "Pinocchio," Jiminy Cricket says "Whoa Nellie!" For the longest time she called her sister, "Hannah Nellie Nichole."

The remainder of the time at the agency is a blur, but I distinctly remember the car ride afterwards. Since our daughters were born in a different state, we had to wait until the Interstate Compact Agreement was signed between the two states before we could take the baby home. We drove over two hours to stay with friends until that paperwork was signed.

I sat in the back seat beside Hannah. I remember staring at her the whole time and feeling numb. I could not wrap my head around the fact that she was my baby. It felt like I was babysitting and would eventually take her back. I remember screaming at myself in my head as I pictured the faces of Megan and Brent. I kept saying, "You need to feel something! You are driving away with that couple's baby. They trusted you, and you need to feel something!" It was awful. I was so angry with myself that I could not look at this tiny face and muster up any emotion.

When we got to our friend's house, I had to plaster a smile on my face. I remember calling my mom and telling her about the meeting with the birth families. She could hear in my voice that I was struggling. When she asked if I was happy, I, of course, told her I was very happy. But I knew that wasn't true. I was angry at me. I felt like I was letting Megan and Brent down.

That night, I was grateful to go to bed. It had been a long day. We had a little basinet for the baby, and I put her down in our room. Shortly after we climbed into bed, I heard this terrible noise. I knew immediately what it was. I jumped out of bed and flipped on the light. The baby was covered with throw up. Not spit up. The whole contents of her bottle throw up. She was gasping a little bit and it scared me to death. I quickly picked her up and held her close, patting her tiny back until she was breathing normally again. I cleaned her while Wayne cleaned up the mess. I was too afraid to lay her back down, so I went into the living room to rock her. With everyone in the house asleep, this was the first time I was alone with the baby. I sat and rocked her as I fed her another bottle. After she fell asleep, I laid her lengthwise down my legs and held her little head in my hands. I gazed at her, the same way I had at the agency that morning when she was first placed in my arms. I was studying every little part of her; her eyelashes, her little rosy cheeks, her very long fingers, and the sweet shape of her face. As I was intently gazing at her, she suddenly smiled in her sleep and broke out into a giggle. I was stunned. This tiny newborn was giggling. In that instant and with that giggle, it was as if something broke through the wall that I was struggling behind. My heart leaped out of me and wrapped around this beautiful daughter of mine. I pulled her to my chest and sobbed. I rocked her for a long, long time. I wasn't interested in going back to bed. All I wanted was to breathe in this little one and cradle her close. As I held her and cried, I thought back over the day, to Megan and Brent and the rest of her birth family. As I snuggled her, I tried to give her enough love from all of us. I knew as I held her they were missing her. I hoped that somehow they would know that she was cherished, and that we always remembered that we were blessed beyond compare two beautiful times now.

Our little Hannah was such an angel. She was the final bit of glue that melded our family together. She was mellow and laid back and very sweet but, at times, could be very spunky.

Her adoption was set up a little bit differently than her sister's. We agreed to write each other once a year until Hannah turned 18. After that, we would have the opportunity to meet again, if all parties agreed. We have loved this correspondence. Hannah has loved it so much as well. She looks forward to her birthday when she knows she will be getting a letter and, in most recent years, gifts from her birth families. She loves them all so much and likes being able to feel connected to them.

Throughout their lives, Katelyn and Hannah have been very close. Katelyn always says that her favorite person in the whole wide world is her sister, Hannah. It has been an honor to love and raise these two amazing daughters with the knowledge that their birth families were counting on us.

This past year, there have been new developments with Megan and Brent. While our adoption dictated that we write letters once a year through the agency, we decided, with the invent of social media, to ditch the adoption agency as a middleman and start to converse with one another online directly. I love seeing updates on these two families and being able to show Hannah what is going on in their world. They also get to see glimpses of us daily. I believe that when we meet them again, face to face, it will feel comfortable and natural.

People are truly amazed at how open we are about our adoption experiences. We (the girls included) are very comfortable talking about it and even love to share our stories with other people. Adoption is beautiful. I feel very privileged that this was the way that God intended our little family to come to be. I wouldn't change it for anything.

WAYNE'S STORY

It finally happened! A baby for us! A perfect little bundle nestled in a Christmas stocking. That is what I saw as we were directed into the softly lit room to meet our daughter, Katelyn. Now we were a family — we were whole. It is hard to express the feelings I had during those times, other than I was just letting it all soak in. Watching Leanne feel the joy and gratitude for our long-awaited blessing was a journey of itself. To see her finally be able to be a mom was a joy to watch.

When Hannah came to us, our family was complete. Being the second baby, I was able to garner more time with her as an infant. Leanne was more willing to share the second time around.

I immensely enjoyed playing with the girls when they were little. Wrestling and tickling were the norm. I also liked to play guitar on their tummies, which induced

squeals and giggles. Instead of a horse, I was the "bear."
The girls would climb on my back, and I would rumble
around or crawl up the stairs to take them to bed. They
loved that for as long as they were small enough for me
to carry them both. They were young teens before that
game ended. I think they found hilarity in seeing me
struggle to carry the both of them. Being a dad to help
guide them as they grew up was a wonderful opportunity to watch them grow into beautiful young women on
the inside and out. I couldn't ask for better girls.

My overriding theme, as the years have gone by, is the
gratitude I feel for the birth mothers. As I have pondered
over how my family came to be, it is hard to describe
adequately what these birth mothers did for us. Sure,
they gave us a baby to raise, but it is much more than
that. The sheer magnitude of what they did can only
be alluded to. Making the decision to place their baby
with another family is perhaps the most difficult thing
a person can do. How does one fully comprehend their
selfless sacrifice? I've thought of that often, and it gives
me a larger sense of the eternal immensity of love and
thankfulness I have for these two birth moms. It has
been a joy to see how they have come through it all,
richly blessed in their own lives in large part due to the
loving decision they made to help my family come to
be.

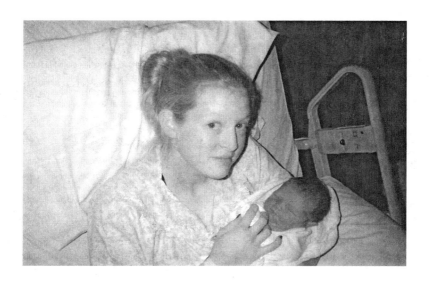

CHAPTER 7
It's a Girl

By sheer, insane willpower, I persevered. Somehow I kept up superior graces with both employers, maintaining an agonizing work schedule that kept me out of the house from 5:15 a.m. - midnight most days, with a short break to drive from one job to the other.

I was living at home with my parents and had no idea when those plans might change. I'd almost completely given up on the idea of going to college since the one school I wanted to go to, Ricks College in eastern Idaho, didn't accept my application. (Yeah, yeah, I'm sure it was divine intervention since I applied when I was PREGNANT, but I was still devastated, neverthe-less.) It was almost like I was waiting out a storm, but I didn't have an umbrella, or a poncho. No, it was like I was in this thunderous, raging storm wearing a copper jumpsuit.

Every single day I wondered how I was going to get past this. I could not picture a happy ending. I didn't know what to do with myself. Hiding away from everyone I loved was awful. I felt lonely and isolated.

Even though I shared a room with my sister, I rarely made time to talk with her or be around her. She and I were the closest of all my siblings. When we were younger, we would stay up late playing Scrabble or Parcheesi, often while eating corn chips with "dip," (i.e. a giant tub of cottage cheese with ranch mix). Our room must have stunk to high heaven. We'd also keep each other entertained by singing popular TV jingles or "Power Tunes" together but *slightly*, intentionally off key. I missed those days of innocent nonsense.

I was so ready for this to be over. Amid the general daily mental anguish I was experiencing in my waking hours, during the final couple months of my pregnancy, I started having these incredibly vivid and horrifying nightmares. One that was recurring for a several week stretch was particularly disturbing. I would be out in public places in these dreams; common places like church, a friend's house, a movie theater. Suddenly, I would hear the sound of a baby crying. I'd look down at my stomach and see the shape of a baby pushing against my skin, like it was trying to get out, and the crying was coming through my own skin. In those dreams I would try to quickly excuse myself and bounce around in the hallways holding my belly and shushing, anxiously trying to calm the baby.

Freaky. I know. I remember it. I still shudder at the thought.

I woke from one of those dreams abruptly one time when I was starting to wet the bed. I caught myself, and hurried to the bathroom. It was here that I caught my own reflection and realized my face and hair were soaked with tears. I wonder if I had been crying out loud in my sleep. It was a rare morning I was off work, and by the time I'd awakened, it was bright daylight outside, around 9 a.m.

After I cleaned myself up, I barricaded myself in my bedroom and told my mother I was sick and needed to go back to sleep. Instead, I lay on that top bunk, eye-level with the window that faced out the front of our house. I stared out the window for a long time with rare, but intentional, blinks. I was on my left side, with my left arm bent and tucked under the pillow as my head pressed heavily on it. My right hand was tucked between my thighs, causing my forearm to rest on my belly. The baby shifted and I felt a push against my arm.

My eyes filled with tears, and I kept staring out to the street. It was going to be a long day with no work interactions.

At some point I pulled out the Game Boy that Brent had given me, and I completed Super Mario Bros. Twice.

It was too warm in my room. I didn't have any covers on and I'd pulled my shirt up a little bit to air out my skin. My mom popped in to check on me and I quickly, (and I'm sure VERY casually) pulled my shirt down to my hips. She asked how I was feeling, and reached up and playfully patted my belly and said, "Why are you getting so tubby?" I ignored it and changed the subject entirely.

Days dragged on. Summer faded into fall, and, on top of my two jobs, I ended up starting college. I enrolled at Boise State just in the nick of time before registration cut off. I made it a few weeks into the semester before I finally went into labor.

It was in the middle of the night when my abdomen was taken over by steady, increasingly painful cramps. I found myself curled on the floor next to the bathroom door. My parents were on a vacation to the Oregon Coast. Only my sister was home, sound asleep on the bottom bunk.

I thought, "This is IT! This is the night I die!"

I hate asking for help. I'll do everything myself before I'll reach out to someone else because I assume it will be a burden to others. It was no different even in what felt like a life or death situation.

The contractions got worse and worse, and finally, through tears, I called out in desperation for my sister and told her I needed her to take me to the hospital. She looked at me in a panic and yelled, "What's wrong?"

"The baby is coming soon."

We scrambled to get to the car, and off we went. Only when we got close to the hospital did we realize we'd both left without putting our glasses on. Neither of us could see what the signs said as we pulled into the hospital, yet somehow we managed to park and head into the first door we could find.

I was lying there on the gurney in triage with my sister, completely shell shocked as she could suddenly see how pregnant I was. Literally, as if it had JUST appeared that day. She sat in a chair next to the bed, eye-level to this giant belly of mine, assiduously filling out a stack of paperwork for me on a clip chart.

The thought of adoption hadn't really crossed my mind as a practical option until I was actually IN the hospital holding a newborn baby. Sure, the word crossed my mind many times, and Brent tried to bring it up a couple of times, but I had no interest in talking about anything with him. He tried to convince me to tell our parents a few times, and I refused even to have a conversation about doing so. It had always been out of the question.

Now, here I was in a hospital draped in the standard-issue pink robe. It was real. It wasn't a dream. I labored for only a couple hours more. It gave my sister just enough time to call Brent and calmly, sternly inform him that he better get down there. He made it with little time to spare before I needed to start pushing. He wanted to hold my hand. I had other plans.

I clasped his hand with my left, and then clawed the length of his forearm with my right. My goal was to draw blood, though I don't recall if I was successful. I can't say for sure if I was screaming out loud at him, or if that was in my mind, too. There was a lot of cussing, so I hope it was mostly internal dialogue.

The clock struck 8:58 a.m. "It's a girl!"

Holy moly. It's a girl. And she's crying. A living, breathing, screaming human just came out of my body. It was overwhelming. I felt overjoyed and terrified.

Then I held this perfect, fully-formed, beautiful little baby in my arms. Her big dark eyes stared back at me. They checked her vitals and then mine. The nurse made friendly small talk and was asking me simple, standard questions. Small talk, while I sat there in a trance. I could feel tears welling up in my tired eyes, the moisture causing the slightest burn. "She isn't mine." I said in a calm tone, almost a whisper. I cleared my throat to speak again. "I can't keep this baby, she isn't mine." I managed to push out with more conviction. She smiled and shifted the conversation. "Oh, you're placing her for adoption? That's wonderful!" She started asking me about the adoptive family as if that had been pre-arranged and seemed very caring and interested in it.

The moment I finally realized that adoption was a REAL option, I had a moment of peace and clarity. I knew that somehow I was going to survive this, and so would this little adorable creature I'd grown so quietly in my belly.

My eldest sister, Erin, who lived just a few minutes from the hospital, was notified. When she heard Shannon say, "Megan just had a baby," she was certain she hadn't heard correctly. Shannon repeated that yes, she is at the hospital with Megan, and yes, she just had a baby.

The adoption agency was contacted from the hospital and within hours, someone rushed down with a giant stack of profiles to look through. I started to pick through them. I was on a mission. I prayed for guidance. I felt a glimmer of excitement creeping out from under the months of fear and despair. I looked at photos of the families. I'd read a couple of lines of each of them and could tell rather quickly that I needed to move on to the next one.

When I came upon this one profile, in particular, my heart jumped. Within the first paragraph I knew I found them. A little family, with one adopted daughter so far, who was just like how I wanted to be when I grew up. They loved music, the outdoors, AND they drove a Jeep. As I read the one-page bio, I thought, "*Yes!*" This is it. But, just to be sure, I skimmed through a few more. I excitedly returned to their story, looked at their smiling faces, and knew they were my daughter's family.

Erin sat with me while I flipped through the files. She pointed out several families that she thought seemed great, but I remained adamant that I had found the right family.

My parents were contacted via cell phone from the hospital. My sister left them a message that said I was in the hospital, as they were out of range in the mountains of eastern Oregon, already making their way back to town after a week away on vacation.

My mother was consumed by overwhelming consternation as the words came through the voice message. She instinctively headed to the hospital in disbelief. She thought maybe she'd misunderstood. Megan is in the hospital? She considered other options. Maybe I was into drugs and overdosed on something. But a baby? Impossible.

She describes it as an out-of-body experience; walking into a hospital room where her daughter sat in a bed holding a newborn baby. She looked around to observe that Brent had invited several friends to hang out. Once the baby had been born, he figured the secret was out and spared no hesitation to invite his buddies over to see the baby, without ever asking if that was okay with me. They were gathered around, talking about the activities of their busy day of high school, without a care in the world, and wolfing down a pizza they had brought along with them.

I tried hard to ignore all of the unwanted company in the little hospital room. I didn't understand why Brent was broadcasting the news of what had happened. Having people come and see the baby and intrude while I was trying to keep a level head about making a responsible decision for the future of this child and, for both of us, made me instantly resentful of him. They didn't think to excuse themselves when my parents arrived, but I had had enough. I needed time with my mother.

There weren't many words exchanged, but there were lots of tears, and plenty of love.

Later, Brent's sister came to the hospital and brushed my hair, finishing it into a braid. She told me that she felt so bad that she didn't know what was going on, and admitted she hadn't been a big fan of mine. She thought I was a bad influence on her little brother. Maybe so. Blame at that point is neither here nor there. She smiled and wanted to express her support for me; for us. I appreciated the gesture, and who doesn't love having their hair brushed?

The adoption agency sent in a young birth mother that first night at the hospital to help me through the process. She sat by my bed while I held the baby. She had only placed her baby a few months prior, and she was an absolute wreck. Within a few moments of telling me about her adoption story, she broke down in tears, wailing, "I miss him so much! I think of him EVERY. SINGLE. MINUTE."

I found myself talking her off the ledge and reassuring her that everything would be okay, and that I was sure she made the right decision for her baby. In my mind I was yelling, "WHAT THE HELL IS THIS?!?! GET THIS CRAZY WOMAN OUT

OF MY ROOM, I DON'T NEED SOME TEENAGER MELTING DOWN. THIS IS NOT HELPING."

The only time I started to slip into a bit of a panic about whether or not I was making the right decision was during her visit. I did not want to end up like that a couple of months down the road. I politely gave feedback to my social worker that they should be more cautious about screening their "support" systems.

The next day, when I could finally walk, Erin helped bathe me in the hospital. I felt completely exposed, and not just because I was buck naked. She lovingly kept my tired, food and sleep deprived body upright while the hot water poured over me. I was amazed that I could have made such a big mistake, and sinned so profoundly in breaking the Law of Chastity, yet here was another sister, serving me with not one ounce of judgment. I was thrilled that one by one, family members still loved me as they discovered what had been going on all these months.

There was a brief discussion, while we were still in the hospital, about whether I should go through with the adoption. Erin considered taking the baby herself to raise with her two young boys, one only seven months old, the other due to turn two the following month. A task I could never have asked of her.

The social worker commended Erin for being there, signifying that a supportive family is surprisingly uncommon. He questioned her outside my room about whether or not I understood the magnitude of the decision I was making. They entered the room together, and he asked me if there was any chance that Brent and I could get married. Without hesitation I replied that no, marriage was not a possibility. Brent was there in the room, standing by, observing.

While filling out various forms at the hospital before we could be discharged, Brent and I decided on the name Emma Faye McCaleb. I picked Emma, he picked Faye, and I'm sure I just wrote my own last name down without consulting him because I earned it, dang it. In the end, it didn't matter. She was named Hannah. Her parents asked if I was cool with that name, as there was another "Em" in the family, her cousin "Emily." I told them I was just fine with that, although truthfully it took me a couple years to finally embrace it.

After two nights at St. Luke's, I headed home, while my baby made her way into the arms of a nice woman who cared for infants waiting to be placed in adoptive homes.

I had been admitted to the hospital weighing in at 138 pounds. I weighed myself at home a few days later—112 pounds. I was frail and exhausted. My body was completely maxed out, and I feebly toddled around the house on my rail-thin legs. My chest was in pain. My own emotions triggering the letdown of milk that I was forbidding to come. I layered three sports bras to keep the lactation at bay.

Things moved fast. Within days I was at the adoption agency, waiting with my parents in one room. She was born on September 29, 1999. She was adopted October 3rd. I held this tiny baby close, taking my time to breathe her in. She was so peaceful. As I held her, she looked up at me, and we shared an unbroken gaze as she completely blew out her diaper. I dutifully went to work changing her, with the help of my mother. Her pink jammies were smattered in poo. I took that as her clever way of letting me know I wasn't ready to be a mother.

My mom took a few photos of me holding her. The social worker came in to let me know the family was there, and they were ready to meet Brent and me. They were absolutely the most perfect couple. Their presence was warm and welcoming, the room filled with love. We talked for a while. While I don't remember the details of the conversation, I was staring at them and taking in their faces and voices, because I knew I wouldn't see them again or hear them speak for many years.

Katelyn, her new older sister, was roaming around, eagerly waiting for the baby. I was grateful to have felt so much joy and energy in the room. I needed that reassurance that this was the right choice.

I went back to the room where my baby was. I held her one last time and cried.

The time came when I had to hand the baby to the social worker. We walked into the foyer together, just outside of the room where her new family was waiting. The image of her in the arms of the social worker is burned in my mind. I told her good-bye and said, "I love you." I kissed her face. He turned and headed down the hall.

We gathered our things and left.

My parents and I went to Pizza Hut immediately after leaving the family services office. What else do you do after a life-changing event like this occurs? You have to move on with regular old, normal, everyday steps. Just saw your baby for the last time? How about some deep-dish pizza? So, we crossed the street and ate some pizza. I cannot remember a single word that was spoken.

I concluded that I needed to document the photos and paperwork from this experience. I ambitiously took up scrapbooking, carefully trimming photos and pressing together collages with stickers onto beautiful pastel pages I bought in the craft aisle at Walmart. That lasted about two and a half pages before I admitted another truth of mine. I'm not good at scrapbooking, and I don't like scrapbooking. Instead, I remained true to myself and grabbed a three-ring binder from my old high school supplies, some clear sheet protectors and just filed away each important item; the birth certificate, the page with her little footprints stamped on it from the hospital, and each set of letters and photos sent to me by Wayne and Leanne during the months following Hannah's placement.

I always looked forward to the letters and stack of photos. I admired the effort it took for these wonderful adoptive parents to pause their busy life and take the time to send me notes of reassurance about how Hannah was doing. Such careful measures to ensure I wasn't worried about my choice. I soaked up every word. I tried to imagine being in their shoes. I loved reading about how much Wayne and Leanne cared for each other. Hearing the honesty in the ups and downs, with the steady undertones of positivity and love they directed toward each other, was more reassurance than even hearing about how Hannah was doing.

It had always been a goal of mine to find the love of my life, and to have a relationship that was so firmly secured with love that there could be no room for doubt, even throughout the rough patches that any couple would undoubtedly experience.

I prayed for Wayne and Leanne to continue having a strong relationship. After all, that was an important reason I thought adoption was the best option for me. I could select a couple who had it all together. They were in love and dedicated to each other's happiness and always put the other person first. They were in it for eternity. I watched intently for those indicators that their relationship was on sure footing. They've made it almost 30 years now. So far, so good.

CHAPTER 8
Moving Forward

I went to the courthouse alone. I wanted to. I needed to.

Only four days had passed since she was placed in her parents' arms.

As I sat on the stand with a judge and my case-worker, Brian, by my side, I stared across the room. Brent sat next to his mother. The room felt enormous, and empty. I could see the look in his eyes. Pleading for me to change my mind. To stay with him. To make a little family and move forward together. He didn't blink, but, after a moment, I couldn't even see him through the pool of tears in my eyes.

How could he do this to me? He was the reason I was in this mess to begin with. How could he ask this of me in the final moments?

I turned my attention back to the situation at hand. I mopped up the flow of tears. Systematically, the judge read through my rights as a mother that I was forfeiting. She firmly, sternly, asked me again if I understood what I was doing, and that by signing that document I would be locking in my decision and *could not change my mind*. I nodded my head and forced out a raspy, whispered, "Yes."

Pen, timidly to paper, I scrawled my name across the thin line at the bottom of a page filled with fine print.

The afternoon was mild. I sat on a bench with Brian and stared up into the overcast skies. Brian was a slim, jolly fella. I wondered how he was old enough to have any college degrees. His baby-face charm seemed just like so many of the guys I'd seen returning from their missions. Clean cut. Dark brown hair combed in a classic missionary do, a side part, and just enough product to give his hair that stay-in-place shine. His soul was filled with enthusiasm. I appreciated the smiles and positive outlook. I trusted him, and he respected that trust. I remember him reassuring me that my life was going to be okay. I was going to be okay. I had done an amazing thing and handled it well. His pep talk was well worded, and just the right amount of optimism, while still acknowledging the magnitude of the day's events.

Before the baby was born I'd already attended almost a month of college. I missed less than a week of school to give birth to a child and make a life-altering decision for us both. Two days after Hannah was placed, I was back at school. A few friends asked where I was, was I okay? I quietly, casually mentioned I wasn't feeling well and was in the hospital for a couple days, but that I felt fine now and was happy to be back.

Even in big lecture halls filled with 350 students, I felt so alone. My mind stirred with much of the same thought processes it had the spring before in high school. Everything seemed so normal in class. People had regular, anticlimactic conversations about their weekend plans. For several weeks I would go to my classes and think about how completely insignificant everything was. I felt like I was wasting my time. My head wasn't in a good place for school, but I did my best to stay on task.

But, how was I supposed to fall into a new pattern of normal life? I no longer knew what "normal" was.

How was I supposed to leave this experience behind?

When we get a cut, we bleed. It scabs over and we heal. What a miraculous thing this body of ours is! We are taught when we are young, "Don't pick at it!" If you pick and pick at the scab, it cannot heal, and you are left with a scar. An ugly little reminder of your wound.

I took this concept literally and bottled up a lot of what I was feeling after the adoption. I didn't want to be an emotional wreck all the time, or bother people with talking about my baby. I felt good about my decision, but I still thought about Hannah every single day, and would every single minute for many months. It was a little odd to me to feel so good about how everything turned out, but still feeling like I needed to be very selective with whom I would share my story.

My own family had been a great support through it all. One by one I had a chance to talk with all five of my siblings. My older brother, Gavin, called me from Brigham Young University, where he was attending. I received letters from my step-brother, Jason, and step-sister, Chelsie. And, of course, my other sisters, Erin and Shannon, had already been in the thick of it. All of them expressed how much they loved me and that I was such a good example to them. Who, me? I recalled a line from the patriarchal blessing I'd received just a couple years before that, regarding my role in the family that said, "The Lord intends that you be an example for good, and even though you are the youngest, without your knowledge, your examples will be followed, and you should be aware of your actions, that you do not destroy the faith and confidence they have in you and in each other."

How could they have so much love for me now? It was such a spiritual experience for me and a testimony of love and forgiveness from them. I thought about how nice it would have been to know how much my family loved me throughout the process of the pregnancy, but what an incredible thrill it was to be the beneficiary of unconditional love from the people I adored the most. There was no judgment. That was the first of many learning moments wherein I discovered it wasn't necessarily about the choices we make, but how we navigate our choices that have the lasting influential impact.

I realize not everyone is that lucky, to have a family who swoops in to support, and my heart hurts for those who are pushed away by family and friends when they hit tough times or make bad decisions. Tangent: If you have someone in your life who you pushed away because of their bad choices, why don't you take a breather from reading this and give them a call to tell them you love them? You will be glad you did.

My healing process was as good as could ever be expected from this situation. I think, on a subconscious level, I began navigating the grieving process while I was still pregnant. *Denial* and *anger?* Check. Those were in full swing early on in my pregnancy. *Bargaining* came toward the tail end of the pregnancy. It was mostly between God and me. It was a pretty common conversation that I had with Him expressing that if, somehow, I lived through this, that I would never break a single commandment EVER AGAIN. I begged and pleaded with Him. I cried and yelled at Him. But, even when I had fits and tantrums, usually alone in my car in a parking lot somewhere, I felt like this was something I was supposed to experience. I would somehow survive, and this would be a prominent part of my life's story.

I resented the moments I felt peaceful. I didn't understand how that was possible in that circumstance to feel any hints of calm, but every so often, they made themselves known.

After I left the adoption agency without my baby, I entered into a new awareness of my reality. I would potentially never see that child again. I hoped that everything would be smooth according to our adoption arrangements, but it all happened so fast. In being really honest with myself, I didn't completely understand all the details of my particular adoption because of how quickly it all happened. I had been in this lonesome void for all these months, and then, in less than one calendar week, the baby was born and she was heading away with another family.

I grasped the very basics. I clung to what little I did know. I had a lemon yellow sheet of paper with a border of bubbly hearts along the edge that explained the parameters of what types of communication and gifts were allowed. It was a semi-open adoption, and all photos, gifts, and letters would be sent via mail. No in-person contact until the child's 18th birthday, if all parties wish to have that reunion.

Eighteen years. That was twice my age! *Depression* began to settle in. I thumbed through a folder of pamphlets and a pastel-colored packet of papers with information on how to navigate the stages of grief, and how to ask for help from friends and loved ones. More well-intentioned papers with smiling bunnies and butterflies, cheerful borders of stars, hearts, flowers, and swirls. Lots of little pictures that looked like they belonged in children's books, not on the tools I'm supposed to use while mourning the separation from my child.

I intentionally pushed forward each day, trying to be positive. Trying to embrace and accept my decision. A true feeling of the *acceptance* stage came when I realized that I was able to be a tool in God's hand through all of this. Despite the whirlwind I'd just experienced, I felt a steady reassurance that I had been a part of something grand. Something profound. Something I would understand even better when I would, years later, bring my own children into this world.

I spent a lot of time loitering in a mix of depression and acceptance. My brain knew I needed to move forward, and I was encouraged pretty quickly (like, the very next Sunday), after all of this came to light, to go see my Bishop at church. Growing up as a Latter-day Saint, I had always been told that I was supposed to repent when I sinned. And, I had sure gotten myself into a pickle this time. Off to the Bishop's office I went.

He asked me a lot of what I assume to be standard questions about what sins exactly I'd committed. There was one obvious one. It all felt very routine. We continued through the process of my confession of sins, but I struggled to answer when asked how I felt about it. I felt sorry for having pre-marital sex, sure, but what I had just been a part of, what I had just experienced by providing a wonderful home for a newborn child of God, and bringing immeasurable joy to Hannah's family was incredible. I didn't feel sorry for that. I couldn't. I was absolutely astounded that I had gotten to become a literal tool in God's hands. I wasn't sorry at all for what this experience had become. I couldn't wrap my brain around repenting for that, but the discussions in that office were hasty and blurry.

I believe my bishop may have been well intended. He had a lot on his plate, as all leaders in ministry do. He gave his best effort to herd his sheep toward the path of righteousness. I like to believe he cared about me. But I felt a lot of pressure to "move on" from this, and *leave it in my past*. The mistake was done, and I needed to repent and be forgiven through the power of the Atonement of Jesus Christ. But, every way that it was explained to me, sounded like this chapter of my life was closed and done, that I needed to straighten up, hold to the iron rod, and begin preparing myself for marriage. And hurry, before there are no young men left!

I met with the Bishop three, maybe four times. I remember leaving one meeting feeling very discouraged because I had already lost my virginity, and it seemed as though he thought there was an inevitable risk that I was just going to go out and sleep with anyone and everyone. Each visit, the conversation always moved toward how quickly I could get married. I needed to find someone who would be compassionate enough to accept me as I was. I felt less healing in those meetings and more like my worth and respectability were on trial. Surely, SOMEONE out there could love me, *baggage* and all?

My mind was still young and impressionable enough that I relied on my church leaders and didn't want to run into any other questionable situations down the road. We buttoned up our meetings, and I guess I was forgiven. At any rate, my Bishop meetings concluded, and everyone started moving forward. I felt like a timer was slapped on my back to hustle into the next phase of life. I didn't like feeling like this part of my life was finished, or that I shouldn't keep talking about all that had happened.

In keeping up my faith that everything would eventually work out, I clung to my fragile, budding testimony, and set my radar to husband hunting.

"Where I Belong"
Original Lyrics by Hannah Nichole

I've often wondered, if I'll ever figure it out

This wall of confusion that confines me

I've got to break it down, there's so much in life
that needs to be found

Makes me wanna work harder, makes me wanna
run faster,

'til I'm right where you are and I'm safe in your
arms and I'm right where I belong,

I'm where I belong.

There'll be times when I wonder if what I'm doing
is actually right,

I'll have to walk the roads; I know I won't be alone

With the hope that you give me, I know that
you're leading me home

Makes me wanna work harder, makes me wanna
run faster,

'til I'm right where you are and I'm safe in your
arms and I'm right where I belong,

I'm where I belong.

They tell me that I can't do anything worth anything at all,

And they say that they know everything, but they
don't know anything at all.

Makes me wanna work harder, makes me wanna
run faster,

'til I'm right where you are and I'm safe in your
arms and I'm right where I belong,

I'm where I belong.

CHAPTER 9
Where I Belong

How did any of us get here? By some random series of events, or by careful design? My life could have taken a number of different paths, and I feel like I'd have been just as happy with different outcomes. I never believed there was just that ONE person for me. I'd find my soulmate, somehow, on a planet with billions of people? Psssh. That seemed silly. I am sure I could have been perfectly compatible with a number of different people. And that's not to say that I wasn't thrilled to have met my husband, but it just keeps things in perspective for me that our choices are not limited, and that we have the power to choose, the ability to create the lives we want.

In the fall of 2000, about one year after Hannah was placed for adoption, my mind was racing about what my future would hold. At the time, I felt like I had limited options. In one respect, I felt like I was damaged goods, and I was worried that I wouldn't be able to find a man who was strong religiously and morally who would still be interested in marrying me. I'd been dating my now husband, Mike, off and on that year, and his uncertainty about marrying me made me question my own worth. Many years later, I would learn that it wasn't because of ME that he had uncertainties. He was battling his own world of demons that I would only be made fully aware of years later, but that is a story for another time.

During the on-again, off-again status I maintained with Mike, I wanted to put so-called, "fate" to the test, and try to figure out what I was destined to do with my life. Because I'd chosen to place my baby for adoption, I had the freedom to make choices for myself and my own future. I took care of her the best way I knew how, and it almost felt like I was being given a second chance at life, and I didn't take that for granted. I was still young, and the whole world was ahead of me. Which road was I supposed to take so that she would grow up to be proud of her birth mother?

The dreams of traveling the world and becoming a famous entertainer of some sort (preferably ending up on *Saturday Night Live*) were fading into my past. I was torn between chasing big dreams of stardom or jumping into a responsible job with a pension plan.

One brisk afternoon in October, I sat myself down and turned in two job applications. One was to interview in Phoenix, Arizona with Southwest Airlines to become a flight attendant, the other was with Washington Mutual Bank as a regional "float" teller. As I clicked "submit" on the painfully slow internet connection in the office tucked in the basement of my parent's house, I felt I sent my fate out into the universe, and was waiting for the answer to present itself. Whichever of these potential employers called first would be the sign of the path I needed to take.

I'd mentioned to my biological father that I might be flying down to a job interview in Phoenix. He'd been living in that area since he left all those years ago. I was excited to get to spend some time with him and get to know him as an adult. He didn't know yet about the baby, or if he did, he didn't say word one about it. Although, I was still on his insurance plan when I'd given birth, so I assumed the words "labor" and "delivery" must have been on a billing statement somewhere at some point.

Just days after I submitted the applications, the phone rang. I grabbed at the corded phone off the wall in the kitchen where my mother and stepfather were sitting at the table just an arm's length away. They listened in as I completed a telephone interview with the Regional Administrator from the bank. I nailed it. She wanted to meet me again in a couple days for an in-person interview, which also went incredibly well, despite wearing bright multi-colored tights and my standard Laura Ingalls braids. Personality and work ethic trump my immature looks.

That was it. I accepted the job that day. I heard from Southwest Airlines less than a week later, but declined to travel down for their interview process. My fate was sealed. The bank called first. The confidence and pride expressed by my sweet parents that day in the kitchen confirmed that I needed to make the most of this new experience, work hard, and chart this course for a respectable life in my new career.

I had come face to face with another pivotal moment, and I boldly moved forward. I was ready to see what the future me was capable of.

In a constant quest of figuring out how to fit in, how to be who we are destined to be, we often get swept up in repeat questions that might seem like they aren't ever clearly answered. Where do I belong? How do I know I am in the right place, that I made the right choices? If I made a bad choice, where do I go from here? Is all hope lost?

I've learned that no matter where we are, that is where we are supposed to be at that moment. Where we *belong* is always changing, it's a moving target. We reach milestones, or sometimes face horrible defeat, and we get to be inside those experiences for those few moments and then it's onto the next thing. It never stops.

Where I am now? A tired mother of three young children and a fourth on the way. Busy trying to build a career as a comedian and an improv trainer (and maybe writer?). A persistently stubborn Mormon woman, constantly pushing the status quo within my own congregation, and breaking down the stereotypes that the world labels us with (which are painfully accurate sometimes). I'm in a whirlwind of living life and working hard right at this moment, hammering out a book about my unplanned pregnancy more than 16 years ago, all the while dealing with the burden of a rocky marriage. Some of these things I choose, and others are thrown into the mix, but either way, I have to work through it all and not question the process.

Where I am now is exactly where I'm supposed to be in this moment. Where I have been and where I will be three, five, or 15 years from now? Those are all places that I belong.

Here's a tip: We have to be active participants in our own life. Savor the successes and work our butts off to move through the challenges. Life cannot be lived from the sidelines. We have to be all in, all the time, and take action if we ever are going to make something of ourselves. We have to be accountable to ourselves. When I got pregnant unexpectedly, I took ownership of the situation. I knew the decision would affect me, this new baby, Brent, my family, and anyone else who ended up in the picture. I couldn't just throw in the towel and give up.

I couldn't let myself be consumed with guilt or regret for what Brent and I had done one fateful, stupidly irresponsible afternoon. Looking back did nothing to help me—I had to look forward.

After a pregnancy, no woman is the same. She is changed forever. I was changed forever. It was time to move forward as the new person I had become.

Just a month or so after they took her home to Washington, I found myself laughing through tears as I read a note that said, "Hannah is a joy—especially when she's not fussy, poopy, or pukey...Ha!" Hmm, ya think? Later in the letter Wayne typed out some parody lyrics to "Copacabana," expressing his hope that I actually knew what song that was. (And, yes, I did. I love Barry Manilow and totally knew every word to that song by high school!) I couldn't believe he took the time to type this up to share with me. "Get out the bongos," he said, admitting that the lyrics might not match perfection, but he had some fun with it. It read:

> *From Boise, we brought home Hannah,*
> *Now she has a cousin named Jana.*
> *With their cousins, when they are silly,*
> *Will name them "ana" banana.*
> *And the family, loving and happy,*
> *It's hard to tell you just how much we feel*
> *And we thank you...*
> *We're so in love...*
> *In the night-time, when she is hungry,*
> *we make up some manna for Hannah,*
> *In a bottle, we rush it to her,*
> *To quiet her little hosannas.*

After eating and she is sleeping,
It's hard to tell you just how much we feel
And we thank you...
We're so in love...

That's it. He's a keeper, Leanne!

I watched Hannah grow from batch to batch of photos that accompanied the letters. They were experts at catching all the best kinds of memories.

Not long ago, I re-read the letter from the adoption profile of the family I selected to raise my child. I didn't remember that I had even kept it, so digging through my black SpaceMaker™ storage tote after many years was a fantastic and emotional time warp to the past. Before I began reading those words, I pulled it out of the plastic sheet protector and held it up. On one side of the heavyweight, high-quality pale blue paper, was a hand-stamped little picture of a watering can filled with flowers at the top center of the front page in purple ink. The other side, another stamp of a heart with swirling vines on either side to conclude their note. The top right corner, an indication that the family was nothing more than a nine-digit case number, like so many other hopeful adoptive candidates.

I was nervous to read it because I remember the wave of certainty that swept over me all those years ago. I'd fully expected to feel that same flood of the Holy Spirit as I sat cross-legged on the floor in my home office, memories laid out all around me. I finally proceeded to read through their letter. "Dear Friend," it began "We wish to extend our heartfelt gratitude for considering us as adoptive parents of your baby. We know that right now you are faced with a very difficult and emotional decision. We know that you wish for your baby the best that life can offer and all of the blessings that Heavenly Father has in store for him or her. As you seek Heavenly Father's help, He will guide and direct you in making the decision that is best for you and your baby. Please know that whatever decision you make, we only wish for you to feel peace and comfort in knowing you are following the direction of your Heavenly Father. He is mindful of you always, and He will bless you as you strive to do His will."

It went on to describe their hopes in adopting a second baby, and expressing deep gratitude for a decision they had to wait for someone to make on their behalf. They already had one daughter, also adopted, and that appealed to me. They love watching old movies, camping, and being in nature. They loved pets, going for drives in their Jeep (also a huge plus in my book), and they were very musical. Wayne, an accomplished pianist and Leanne sang like a songbird. He was in the Bishopric; she was the Young Women's President. They were the kind of people I wanted to be someday with my own husband.

There was something comfortable and stable about the way they described their life. Caring, adventurous, consistent. Nothing flashy, and as my eldest sister mentioned recently, she was impressed that I selected a family who was so normal. I hadn't at all thought of them as *normal* when I read their letter in the hospital. They were anything but. They were perfect in my heart. Before I met them, I could feel it, pounding in my young, fragile heart, that they were something very special, and were about to become a permanent part of my life's story.

It was and is still so incredible to me that when people make the decision to adopt, they go all in and are willing to receive whichever baby comes to them. Boy or girl? Didn't matter to Wayne and Leanne. Their trust in a loving Father in Heaven superseded everything that would come with that difficult process.

I could feel the genuine concern they had for the well-being of the birth mother. Adoption comes along with such a bittersweet reality, wherein they can only become parents if someone, somewhere, bravely chooses to place their baby in an adoptive home and handpicks them from a seemingly infinite pile of prospective families.

As I finished reading their letter, there in my home while my own kids were sleeping soundly in a quiet house, for a brief moment I felt let down that I wasn't overcome by the Spirit. I had expected to be drenched in my own tears by the end of it, but I just held the page in my hand and looked at the words on the paper. That's all they are. That's all they were. Then as I slipped it carefully back into the protective cover it dawned on me. I didn't NEED the Holy Spirit to testify anything to me in that moment. But, knowing that I read that exact same letter so long ago and was completely overwhelmed by emotion and a burning ache in my chest, was in fact a greater testimony to me of the power of that Spirit. I needed that guidance in a very clear and urgent way when I held that newborn in my arms. And I was open to receiving it.

Adoption encompasses so many deep feelings for everyone involved. It is a delicate task that harmoniously brings strangers together and connects them forever with a precious new life. Whether the adoption is closed, semi-open, or wide open, their worlds are connected forever, even if only in their hearts.

At a very young age, my oldest son, Fletcher, started asking questions about where babies come from. Kids are smarter and comprehend way more than some people want to admit. I remember driving home one day in my cherry red Volkswagen Rabbit, sun roof open, sunshine pouring down, and out of nowhere he asked, "How in the heck did I get inside your tummy?" I gave him the basic answer, that moms have tiny baby seeds in their bellies that grow and grow until it's time to come out. "Come out how?" he inquired. "The baby hole," I said. Man, that sounded dumb, but I hoped that would be the end of it. Nope. "But how does the baby seed start growing in there?

It all just magically happens on its own?" he pushed, unsatisfied with my answers. So I went on to a bit more detail that moms and dads have special parts that join together when it's time for that seed to get fertilized, like fruits and vegetables in the garden. Finally, the questions stopped and he stared out the window. He was three.

Around that same time, I started to share things about Hannah with him. He loved hearing about her. Over the years he has increased his understanding of her, and her role in my life—in our lives. In recent years he has gotten pretty upset at me for not keeping her. He wished we could be with her for holidays, and just for everyday activities. He liked telling people about her without me knowing, including some of my in-laws who didn't know about her yet. "I have an older sister in Washington named Hannah. I haven't met her in person yet, but she's pretty rad. We'll meet when I'm 10."

Turns out they had known for a couple years and didn't mention anything to me, waiting for me to share the story on my own.

At one point, Fletcher probed Mike for more information when I wasn't present. He hadn't yet realized that Mike wasn't Hannah's dad. Fletcher wanted more answers as to what mom was thinking when she gave away his older sister. Why weren't WE a family? Mike told him that if I had kept Hannah that he and I might not have gotten married, and that Fletcher and our younger kids wouldn't even exist. Just prior to Fletcher's head exploding at the thought, Mike buttoned up the conversation with a reminder that Mom had been chosen to be a special helper for Heavenly Father to get Hannah to her family because her parents couldn't have babies on their own.

When Fletch recounted this conversation with me, he still seemed a little dissatisfied and asked again, "Why wouldn't I have been born if you kept Hannah?" I explained that Hannah had a different father, and then he busted me for not being married when I had her. Since, as you remember, I explained that it was moms and dads who come together with their magical parts to make babies, and moms and dads are married as far as he knew. He dissected that information himself once he realized that Mike wasn't her father, and that she was born before I had even met Mike.

It was a great teaching moment, and I got to share more about my process with helping Hannah get to the home she was meant for. He is still bummed that we don't get to see her all the time, but he has accepted why it is this way.

HANNAH'S STORY

My parents never sat me down to tell me. I just always knew. I am adopted. I always knew that my parents had tried for years to have kids, but were unable to do so on their own. I always knew that, even though they didn't conceive me, I was, without a doubt, their daughter, and they loved me. Both my sister, Katelyn, and I were adopted as newborns, and we were raised always knowing how we came to be Rickords. My sister's birth mother ended contact when my sister turned five due to the way her adoption was set up, but we knew growing up that we would meet Katelyn's birth mother and her family after she turned 18. My story was different though. I have always had contact with my birth mother, Megan. That is a relationship that I wouldn't trade for anything. We have a semi-open adoption, which means that we have contact through letters, but I won't meet Megan until I am around 18. Most of the 16 years of my life, we have sent annual letters, but in the past year, my mom has added Megan as a friend on Facebook. I remember growing up, there was just about nothing as exciting as waiting for my birthday to roll around so I could get the annual letter. I remember about eight years ago when we heard that Megan had a baby boy. I fell in love with that little dude. Seeing pictures and hearing stories about her life, her family, and her kids is one of my favorite things. I love watching as my two birth brothers and birth sister grow up. I have a very special place in my heart for that family.

This past year, I have noticed the negative connotation attached to adoption. When people hear that I am adopted, they usually follow up by saying "I'm so sorry," "That must be so hard for you," "Wow. You must hate your real mom for giving you away." Why are you sorry? It's not hard for me. Plus, my mom, Leanne, is my real mom, Megan is my birth mother, and no, I do not hate her or my birth father. They made that choice not because they didn't want me, but because they loved me too much not to give me the life that my parents now give me. Sure, there are times I wonder how my life could have been had I not been placed for adoption, but not for a second do I resent being adopted. I'm saddened to see that the overall opinion and view of adoption puts a negative filter on something that I find sacred. I was raised always knowing my story, and always knowing how hard it was for my birth parents to make that choice for me, to place me with a family that could provide for me when they couldn't.

Shortly before my birthday last year, I read the old letters from my birth parents. While reading one from my birth father, I was overcome with emotion. I could feel his love as I read. I keep the contents of that letter close to my heart, but, I also knew in reading those letters that, without a doubt, my birth parents had an immense love for me that is too great for me to fully understand.

They didn't make the decision to place me for adoption to make life easier for them, they made the painstaking decision because they loved me so much.

It is no secret that not every adoption is like mine. I feel so blessed for how things worked out for me, and am sad that not every adoption turns out as beautiful as mine. But I also believe that you can't take the negative adoption stories and blanket all of adoption with them. Adoption is what brought my family together. I have always thought of my birth parents as a train station. They were key to getting me to my destination. They brought me into this world, and placed me with my family. God chose them to be my family.

Growing up, my sister and I shared a book collection. We had books like Charlotte's Web, Skippyjon Jones, and many more. Two of our books were about adoption. I loved those books, and we read them all the time. ("How I Was Adopted" by Joanna Cole and "Tell Me Again About the Night I Was Born" by Jamie Lee Curtis.) We grew up knowing that being adopted didn't make us flawed. The fact that I was adopted is a detail of who I am. To me, it's no different than my brown hair and blue eyes.

I am thankful my history was never hidden from me, and that it was never looked down upon. Because of that, I feel nothing but gratitude toward my birth parents and what they did for me. How could I be ungrateful to the people who showed so much love for me that they could make such a sacrifice? My birth mother carefully and lovingly picked my family. God had His hand in all of this. He had trusted my birth parents to get me to my family, the family that was meant for me all along. Because of this, *I know that I am exactly where I belong.*

CHAPTER 10
Mind Your Own Business

In the spring and summer of 2015, I kept having the thought pop into my mind that I needed to share my story of adoption. By the fourth or fifth time the thought crossed my mind, I realized, perhaps, it wasn't me putting that thought there, and that I should hit my knees on the issue. I prayed for a couple of weeks about it and talked with Leanne, who was also feeling strongly about the importance of sharing positive adoption stories from all angles. I ran it by my husband, a man of very few words, and he didn't indicate anything blatantly against it, so I started to brainstorm on the subject.

Over the course of a couple of months, and after several meetings with a group of close friends, I was ready to proceed. The Spirit was very strong in one particular meeting. One of them asked me WHY I needed to share it, what would be the purpose, the goal? Hearing my own voice express why this story is so important to me made me realize that the story is so much more than *just an adoption.* This story is who I am.

Trials give us a chance to really show and live our true character. Until I started sharing my story with people over the years and hearing their feedback of how remarkable it was, and how the story had inspired them, I hadn't even realized how deeply impactful it was for *me*. But, every decision I made after placing the baby, and decisions I make now, I take very seriously. I chose a very sensible balance of corporate career while still dabbling in my hobbies so I would have things to share with Hannah in my annual letter. This child became my litmus test on many things. Would Hannah be proud of me for doing this? It wasn't always the be-all and end-all with every choice I've made, but I enjoyed having that added layer of accountability to fuel my dreams and hard work.

I spent a great deal of energy working hard, no matter what the job was. I've volunteered hundreds of hours over the years, and I never miss a deadline. I'm reliable and consistent. I'm the one people vent to when they have a bad day, and the one people turn to for comic relief. I always wanted to prove myself even when I didn't have to. It was like this underlying theme in my life, that I had experienced firsthand the heartache and joys of making both really good and very bad choices.

When it finally came time to share this, I knew I had built a very solid reputation with a large number of people who knew me in some capacity. For some reason, having built up credibility in the community gave me a little boost in confidence and validation that the time was right. Those who loved me would still love me, and those who didn't, well, who cares? I was ready to share, knowing that the intent for sharing wasn't about those people anyway. It would be cathartic for me, and it could open doors and opportunities for me to be a support to anyone else who needed it.

Funny how it seems that everyone has all the answers to life's problems when they are on the outside as the observer. I think about a close circle of friends of mine, some of my best friends. We get together for dinner about once a month. Rae, Shauna, Aly, Meg, and me. We do a lap around the table giving updates about the goings on in our lives. It's a safe place to dish all the details. Support and discussions ensue. Often times, our troubles carry over from month to month, or year to year, with very little progress toward resolution. With close friends it is hard to watch. We all look at each other and know how WE would handle things if we were in THEIR situation. Or so it seems.

Once, at the end of dinner, I proposed a concept for a new reality show called, "Problem Swap." Everyone shares their biggest problems with the group, then you pass your problem to the right, and that person just makes all the decisions for you to fix your situation. Poof! Everything is solved and everyone is happy. Just that easy. Har har.

Obviously, it doesn't work that way. Sure, it seems easy, as the observer, to identify the pain points that must be relieved, but for the person living in it, there are many more strings attached, and other things that will be disrupted one way or the other when a big change is made.

Even as a birth mom, I am incredibly cautious about giving advice to other women. It is such a deeply personal and life-changing decision. But, showing love and compassion to another woman as she navigates this process? That, I can do. Lending an ear to hear the words of someone who is troubled can be a very valuable gift. And, by sharing my own story, I can offer my perspective for them to pick and choose what nuggets they want to take from it and apply to their problem solving.

It's no secret that I'm a huge advocate for adoption, but, even more than that, I will fight to ensure every woman has the opportunity to make an informed decision. Any woman who finds herself in the situation with an unplanned pregnancy needs to have the time and space to review ALL options so SHE can be the one to make this permanent decision. There is no going back.

My healing process was as smooth as it probably could have been. And, while it was anything but pain free, my greatest peace came from knowing I was able to make this decision on my own, with Brent offering support the only way he knew how.

But, over the years, even though I was fairly selective about how and when I brought up my story of adoption, responses have been less than helpful, and, indeed, borderline hurtful. If you have never been through it, and especially if you are a mother who gave birth to a baby and you kept that baby, you have no way to even begin to fathom how a woman can choose to place her baby with strangers.

I lost track of the number of times I mentioned to some of my close acquaintances that I had an unplanned pregnancy my senior year of high school and chose adoption, and they retorted, without even trying to filter:

"I could NEVER give away my baby!"

"Oh, I just don't know HOW you could have DONE that."

"I think about my babies and I just love them TOO much, and I could never IMAGINE."

"Not all of MY babies were PLANNED, but I just did what I needed to and HANDLED IT."

...and so on.

These comments are laced with implications that you can relate to what has happened, but you can't. Instead, you suck the beauty of the situation right out of the conversation.

When I hear these types of statements, I know my history affords me the opportunity to shine some light on the topic and to educate people in a loving manner. Rest assured, it wasn't because I didn't LOVE my baby that I chose adoption. I loved her, and still love her deeply, and think of her daily with all the caring and concern my maternal instincts can muster.

I believe, in most cases, people are oblivious to how they are coming across and are actually trying to empathize with the birth mother, but have no idea how to do so appropriately.

I hate to say it, but we, as a species, are awkward and uncomfortable around pain and suffering. It's hard to think of the right words to say. So, when nothing comes, the best you can do is show love and attention, even with a hug or a smile, or a squeeze on the shoulder. These simple gestures can express the desire to care and support another person who is grieving.

MESSAGE TO THE FRIENDS AND FAMILY OF THAT SPECIAL BIRTH MOM IN YOUR LIFE:

Don't be weird! Please understand that birth mothers love to be able to talk about the child they placed for adoption. It doesn't make us feel awkward. It is therapeutic and wonderful when someone takes the time to express even the slightest bit of interest. It doesn't have to be any more forced than when you nod and smile when your friends tell you about all the things their kids are up to.

I wish I had been more open with my family and friends about my feelings as I went through the healing process. I wanted to talk about Hannah every day. Of course I did. I love her. Looking back, I know that nobody ever seemed inconvenienced when I talked about her, or acted put out at all, yet subconsciously I worried that, even if they were being nice, they might have been thinking, "Here we go again," or "Haven't you moved on yet?" I know now that wouldn't have really been what they were thinking. I was lucky to have family who loved me and expressed their love and caring toward me *and* Hannah.

If you know someone who is, at this very moment, in the thick of an unplanned pregnancy, try extending love and patience. It will be for the greater good of everyone if you can help her feel loved and valued every step of the way so that she can live with whichever permanent decision she makes.

And, it's no secret that pregnant ladies tend to find themselves in a pretty sensitive state of mind with emotions running high. Don't take advantage of that vulnerability by interjecting your opinions too firmly. Don't abuse the trust they have in you by trying to influence them to do what YOU would do. They, we, need to feel love and encouragement when we are cookin' up a new life within our own bodies.

Many people have stepped forward to tell me their stories since I first went widely public. I've heard stories from all angles, and even from some men who have been birth fathers, or the silent party when an abortion took place against their will. Many women, of various ages and demographics, have told me about their choices and how they feel about those choices in present day. For some, it haunts them. For others, it is a place of beauty and empowerment. Those who had their decision greatly influenced by other people, however well-meaning they may have been, are stuck in longer periods of grief and regret.

Placing a child for adoption is a difficult adjustment for a birth mom. I spent many hours crying and in complete overwhelm about this life I could feel moving in my body, now in the arms of another mother. While I didn't doubt my decision (often), I still felt a complete void in my heart. I closed my eyes to picture baby Hannah playing, squealing, smiling, crying, sleeping, and even puking. I cherished the very imagination I had of what I might be missing.

You cannot argue with a mother's intuition. Now that I have children of my own, I can hardly believe I am the same person who once placed a baby for adoption. But, just as surely as I held my babies one by one, fresh from the womb, feeling with every nerve in my body that they were my babies, I remember just as vividly feeling from head to toe an overwhelm of love and joy that I got to be tasked with giving the greatest gift of all to Leanne. I could feel the joy, as almost an out-of-body experience, like I was feeling that joy of motherhood as proxy for Leanne, and I hadn't even met her yet.

Is adoption the right answer every time? Of course not! Don't be a goober. Every single pregnancy, though unplanned by the mother, was part of a plan.

But, remembering that keeping a baby just to say you are "taking responsibility" for the situation you got in, isn't the ONLY option to be responsible.

In the world of adoption, things have changed a lot since 1999. I didn't intentionally connect with other birth moms until recently, after sharing my story originally on September 15, 2015. I was blown away by the response of my humble blog post and video, which I posted on Facebook. Eight hundred twenty-four likes, 183 comments, and 102 shares later, I was flooded with private messages and added to a bunch of birth mother groups.

Birth mother support groups are new to me. I went to a few meetings after I placed my baby, but found that the atmosphere was depressing and wasn't helpful to me. So many tears of regret from other women who had made the choice to place their babies. Was something wrong with me? Did I do this wrong? I didn't feel regret. Yes, I missed my baby, and my heart ached for missing out on the tender moments of her childhood, but I knew I made a great choice. I had no doubt that Wayne and Leanne were going to be absolutely incredible parents. I wanted to try and support those women, and still do, but I feel very differently than many of them.

Today, support groups are right online. Many of them are a click away on Facebook. Many of them feel like the room I walked into 16 years ago where women are venting and seeking validation. This is still a good thing, and paramount for women processing their grief.

Oftentimes, in these online chats, people discuss their open adoptions, which have become very popular. I read a lot of stories about them and how wonderful the relationship is, but I know that wouldn't have been the best fit for *me*. I felt confident in Hannah's parents. I trusted them and had complete faith that they would make the best decisions for her without my input.

I put myself in the shoes of prospective adoptive parents. If I couldn't have my own children, then get lucky enough to be selected by someone to raise their baby, but only if I need to let them name my baby, visit often, be a part of every major event, get frequent updates, include them in my decisions about immunizing, feeding, disciplining, etc. I would be completely overwhelmed. Hats off to those who want a baby so much, and have so much love to give that they are willing to have another mother involved with their child indefinitely.

Please understand that I don't think this is *wrong*. It's really the wave of the future of family units in adoption. It is humbling and inspiring to see this huge evolution in the world of adoption.

At the time of my placement, semi-open adoptions seemed perfect for me. There was a promise of frequent letters and photos in the mail during the first year, and continued photo sharing and letters at least once per year until the child's 18th birthday. (Or some arrangement along these lines.) Healing from this experience was going to be hard anyway, but for me, it was just enough contact to see that my daughter was healthy, taken care of, and brimming with smiles.

Seeing how open many adoptions are in recent years, I have found myself wondering from time to time if I had done enough all this time. Should I have sent more gifts? Should I have written more often? Was there a chance that Hannah questioned whether or not I loved her? These questions will eat you alive if you let them.

Shortly after Leanne and I connected via Facebook, per her request, I mentioned to her that I intentionally kept my distance and reserved my contact to once per year around Hannah's birthday so that they would be free to enjoy their lives with their beautiful daughters without me hovering like a vulture, but that recently I have begun wondering if, perhaps, I should have done more.

Thankfully, she reassured me that she and Wayne appreciated that space and distance, and that I could trust that I, in-fact, held a very substantial place in their world. The many times they thought of me and my well-being, and the countless prayers they said on my behalf. Letter after letter, Leanne's heart spilled out onto paper with words that would heal my soul.

"Not a day goes by that I don't think of you. I wonder how you are doing and what you are up to. I especially think of you when I hold and rock Hannah. When I whisper to her that I love her and kiss her on the head, I often whisper it for you, too. I try as hard as I can to give her enough love for both of us."

CHAPTER 11
Not My Plan

Just a couple of stupid kids who had stumbled into a lifelong connection, Brent and me. I've never regretted how things happened. Sure, there were moments along the way when I kicked myself for getting into such a sticky situation, but it needed to happen that way. Brent was nice enough, he always tried to be a cheerful listening ear. When the time came for the reality check about parenthood, the option for adoption became an undeniably perfect option for me; for us. Brent was just starting his senior year. There was nothing about moving into his parent's basement to raise a baby that sounded remotely appealing. It just didn't feel right at all. That wasn't the life I wanted for my kids. We were still kids.

My social worker, Brian, shared with me a message from the LDS Family Services I used for my adoption. "We feel that all children have the right to be raised in a home fit for children, equipped with a mother and a father who can give them the love and care that they need. We encourage unwed mothers to think of their children's well-being over their own desires to raise the children, and put them in a home that they are unable to provide."

"...by giving the opportunity to select the parents of their child, they are less likely to have any regrets after the adoption."

In the short window of time that I had been immersed in this whole adoption thing, I kept reviewing in my brain the logistics that had to occur for some people to become parents. I, like a punk, got pregnant without even trying, while others who long for parenthood may be given the trials of infertility. Seems so unfair, those who cannot bear children on their own rely on someone making a "mistake" that leads them to an unplanned pregnancy, thus providing a way for adoptive hopefuls to become parents if that birth mother determines she is unable to raise the child herself. It is a powerful predicament to consider.

It reminded me of Adam and Eve in the Garden of Eden. In the LDS faith, we are taught that they were commanded to multiply and replenish the Earth, and also commanded not to partake of the fruit of the Tree of Knowledge of Good and Evil; they couldn't fulfill the one commandment until they had broken the other.

As we all know, the fruit was partaken of, "Adam fell that men might be..." and they were cast out of Eden, and, after the way of forgiveness was paved for them to repent of their wrong doing through the Savior they had been provided, "...and men are, that they might have joy." (2 Nephi 2:25) they were able to embark on the task of procreation. And boy, did they learn some big lessons along the way, having the knowledge now, that everything has its opposite.

For me, it is a testimony builder to know that we are not perfect, and we aren't expected to be. Not a single person on this planet, except Jesus Christ, has been or will ever be without sin. But, how we conduct ourselves when faced with adversity, and how we use this new information from the lessons we learn is basically our scorecard. If we keep making the same mistakes over and over, we aren't progressing, but if we can examine our situation and make a choice to obtain the best possible resolution and avoid repeating that same challenge again in the future, we are rewarded spiritually. That kind of growth can't be put on a scale.

My relationship with Heavenly Father has had its ups and downs like any other relationship. Questioning my faith when the trials really hit, that's when I realize why having a testimony of my own is so important. That's where the real growth comes. When Carrie Underwood sang, "Jesus Take the Wheel" she was onto something good. There is freedom in letting go.

If you're like me, sometimes you want to blame others for situations that you have to deal with in life. That will happen. A lot in some cases. But, even within those scenarios, there is room for personal growth if you can gather enough courage to accept it for what it is, and choose to forgive and love the person who hurt you. Some things, we can control. Others, we either have to hold on for the ride or let go altogether. The choice is yours.

When I was in high school, I was a curious young lady, like so many others. The carnal nature of human beings was alive and well. Hiding under the roof of our churches and synagogues only gets us so far. We need to be realistic about the temptations of the adversary having just as strong of a pull on those who faithfully attend church and try their best to choose the right.

I believe in abstinence before marriage. I always did, but I do even more now. Having experienced the repercussions of NOT following that guidance made me understand exactly why that is such a big deal.

I can't think of a single time when the Law of Chastity was taught in my youth, and now as an adult, where it isn't tip-toed around and glossed over because of how uncomfortable it makes everyone. It is one of the most critically important laws we've been given—to protect our bodies and the divine structure of the family unit. Yet, this lesson is notorious for being awkward and taboo. It leaves young people feeling ashamed. I know it did for me. If you remember, I had tested the waters of telling my Mormon friends when I had broken this sacred law, so there was NO WAY I would even consider letting anyone else in on my shameful secret. It was written in my conscience, but the people who preach love and acceptance and living Christ-like lives were the ones I feared would judge me the harshest.

Our bodies, we need to understand, are sacred and beautiful. They are equipped with the tools to create human lives! That is why we must be so diligent in protecting our bodies. My belief is that this is ordained by God, but even if you are into the sci-ence-y explanation of where babies come from, it is an awe-in-spiring act to unite, man and woman, to create another living being with the very cells of your DNA.

Talking freely and confidently about this subject is the only way that we can attempt to protect it and arm ourselves for bat-tle against the enemy. Simply telling young people to be chaste and virtuous will never work if they aren't empowered with the ability to communicate openly on the matter. It needs to be-come a comfortable, normal conversation within our homes and churches.

Modesty is on a rapid decline and has been for a long while. Attempts at modesty are labeled as prudish. Things like body positive movements and catchy hashtags like #FreeTheNipple (which I don't recommend doing a search on) have a global reach and provocative images are celebrated as liberating and promote gender equality. Our genders are not equal. We, men and women, were created to complement each other and to need each other. We have different skill sets emotionally and functionally. That isn't an accident, yet the world would have us believe that, in order to be a confident woman today, we must be EQUAL to men in all aspects. We cannot, because we are not. And, personally, I don't think that is a bad thing.

Many times I feel like I've been under fire in the battle of this mortal life. As we blaze into the war against the evils of our day, sometimes we just have to charge ahead into the unknown and pray that along the way we get hit with the spiritual shrapnel that will stay with us after the dust settles.

We don't always get to choose our battles, though sometimes our experience is a result of a choice we made at some point. Whether we choose them or not, our experiences are part of a master plan. There is a plan and purpose for each of us that is far greater than we can understand. And, we won't be able to see how strong we are until we have made it out to the other side.

The scope of what our common enemy dishes out to us is daunting. My first traumatic experience in life was an unplanned pregnancy. Maybe yours was an illness or a physical handicap. You might have infertility issues, or you've suffered the loss of your own child. Maybe you've been abused, or been the abuser. Perhaps you are struggling with addiction to drugs, alcohol, or Diet Coke. Maybe infidelity and/or pornography. Or, maybe you didn't take that job opportunity, or pick a different major in college, or tell that person, "I love you" before it was too late.

The truth is, we are all going to have struggles. Some of us will feel like we can't catch a break and that the hits "just keep coming." All the "what-ifs" will drive you crazy if you let them. The part that really stinks is that when something really big, I mean REALLY big, is happening in your life, that is your opportunity for the most growth. Those are the times when our faith is put to the test. I admit that there have been times in my life when I've been angry with God and didn't want to believe that anything good could come from terrible situations. But it can, and in my life, I know that the more I push away my Heavenly Father, the worse I feel. I still don't have all the answers, but having a spiritual foundation, filled with faith in something greater than myself, gives me the comfort that I don't NEED all the answers.

Most of the big events in my life seem to happen with very little planning. If I ever own an airline, I'll call it "The Seat of My Pants" because that's how I fly. I've noticed that trend and, good or bad, it's the way I roll so I now embrace it. I, like many young girls, dreamt of the day that I would become a mother. In fact, I had in my mind that I would get married shortly after high school and get right to work on my litter of children.

Just like with my career in comedy, things just happened and I jumped in with both feet—knowing I can't swim. I loved the thought of performing, but I didn't know how to plan for it just perfectly. The very first time I tried stand-up comedy, I was sitting in the audience watching my friend host the open mic in a dark, second-story pub in Meridian, Idaho. I thought I would try learning by watching, but he had another idea. He announced me as the next comic for the night and the crowd, who was oblivious to the fact that I'd never written a joke in my life, clapped and whistled as I took the mic and squinted into the spotlight. I was no stranger to other styles of performance, but this was different. You are supposed to prepare material for stand-up and then pray people laugh at you.

That was not my plan for the night. Thankfully, I didn't dodge the opportunity. Even though I ended up telling some very random, disjointed little stories for what felt like two hours (it was three minutes), I had survived! I even got a few little chuckles from a couple of encouraging gals off to my left. I was happy to take courtesy laughs.

Sometimes we need a little nudge by someone who has more confidence in us than we have in ourselves. And, there is One who will always see that potential buried inside us. I'm grateful for the opportunity I have been given, on many occasions, to forgive myself for my mistakes, and to be made whole through the atonement of my brother, my Savior, Jesus Christ.

CHAPTER 12
This is Not the End

I've spent a lot of time reading through old letters and my journal from the time right after Hannah was placed. As I read my own words, jogging my memory and spurring the accompanying emotions, I couldn't help but feel like I am looking in on someone else's past. How could that have been me? Who is this person? Such careful strokes of the pen, writing as nicely as I could.

It's a very peculiar feeling to remember each moment with such clarity, while also feeling a distinct disconnect to the situation. Looking back, I understand that it had to happen that way. I didn't want to allow myself to feel the emotions connected to carrying a baby.

I remember, as I wrote in that journal, that I intentionally left out details. Details about what activities happened that day, or emotions that I was feeling. I had to bury them deep. At the time I would picture giving that journal someday—many days down the road—to my birth daughter, and I wanted to hand-craft the words she could read. I wanted her to feel like I was stronger than I was. Like I was holding it together, and I didn't want to let my guard down even then.

I wanted her to think I was so brave and to look to me as an example of courage, and I wanted it to be on my terms. My only true regret was not pouring out my soul the way I should have in that journal. I should have let myself break down more. But, perhaps, those private memories of sorrow are for me to hold in my mind and store away safely.

Now, as this book reaches publication, we are entering a new phase of this whole adoption experience. Very soon we'll be meeting in person. The story will keep going on, and new, wonderful memories will be made. More rich blessings are in store for all of us.

When I wrote my usual annual letter to Hannah for her 16th birthday it was different than previous years. We had a closer connection through social media so there was less "stuff" to catch her up on like I typically would in those letters. I pondered a lot. What can I tell her that is going to be of any value, or that she won't see anywhere else? I thought about how old she was. On the approach to dating age! Yikes. Dating? Again, I said, "Yikes."

I found myself dancing in a puddle of irony as I told her, very strictly, to heed my advice and STAY AWAY FROM BOYS! Trust me on this one, I said.

For me to be telling this to the girl whose life sprung from the very fact that I didn't follow that advice, was humorous and also put a bit of a pit in my stomach. If there is one person's advice she should take on the matter though, it's mine!

Fewer than four months had passed since the adoption took place when I met my husband, Mike. I remember the feeling of delight when I first laid eyes on him. I'd been sitting in church with my sister, Shannon, when I saw him walk across the front of the room in Sunday school. He was so handsome. Tall, dark hair, chiseled jaw, and glasses. Very Clark Kent, ladies. He didn't look around much, just went straight for his seat, and had his head down for most of the hour, doodling in a black journal.

Man, it felt warm in there, and not just because the sun was flooding through the windows. I told my sister, "I'm going to marry him someday." Her reply? A typical "mm hmm." Yeah, maybe I'd said that about several attractive fellas during the past couple of months, but this time was different.

I was on pursuit immediately to find out his name. I called his apartment and talked to his roommate for just long enough that he thought I was hitting on HIM. I shifted gears to ask him about Mike. "Ooooooooooohhhh" he said. "No, Mike isn't dating anyone I don't think."

I found out where he worked and tracked him down in the mall and asked him on a date. (Talk about leading the charge for ladies going after what they want, right?)

It wasn't more than a few dates later that we met in his tiny apartment living space to talk. He sat in this ratty old beige recliner in the corner, while I took up roost on the edge of the dark orange corduroy couch closest to him. A brass lamp stood off to the side between us, illuminating the area of the room where we began chatting. I wanted to cut to the chase. I let him know that just last September I had a baby...

There was a steady, controlled look on his face, which must have been him trying to appear as if he wasn't in a panic.

I went on to say she had been placed for adoption. He thanked me for sharing that with him. I expected lots of questions, but he didn't have many. He looked relieved when I didn't follow up the announcement of the baby with "and she's at home with my mom." He still wanted to date me. Success!

He let me know that he was coming out of a very short-lived marriage, and had only finalized the divorce a month prior. I had more questions than he did (I always do), but inside I was thinking, "Whew! We both have baggage, let's get married, already!"

We were perfectly imperfect for each other. I felt lucky to have the attention of such a smokin' hot guy, and we married in May 2001. After 15 years of marriage, we are just barely figuring out how it works, and our story has hit/will hit many devastating bumps, but, we are still trying and that is what counts.

I have pushed forward through the steps of repentance on more than one occasion in my life, and I've felt good about the progress I've made spiritually each time. There is so much learning and changing and healing to do when you tackle life as aggressively as I tend to do. Being real and raw about struggle and all the things that make life so hard, but still having faith and staying the course make me finally feel like I understand what it means to be righteous...something I will continue to strive toward.

Having monumental life experiences is worthless if we don't share them with people who may need help on the journey. It took many years for me to realize that because I lived through a traumatic experience, I had a valuable resource, ME, to share with people who are going through similar situations in present day. Hitting the skids myself has made me so patient and empathetic to others. I've been able to see my own resilience when I take the time to open up to people and let them see the vulnerability.

I wish we could all stop sweeping our mistakes and life lessons under the rug.

I think of the word, *closure*. That word is so finite. As humans, we want closure after something traumatic happens so we can move on. Perhaps, we feel we need that permission to move forward. To close the book on that chapter, figuratively. I believe that having resolution is powerful, but, even more powerful, is when we can wear our experiences as a badge of honor for what we have endured. And, never close a door so tightly on the past that we forget the person we became for having walked through it.

Adoption was absolutely the right decision *for me*, for my baby, and for the incredible adoptive family who had been preparing to be parents LONG before I'd ever become pregnant.

I'm so grateful that I essentially stumbled upon the option of adoption. It was always there, but not explained to me in the matter-of-fact way that I needed to hear, not like the other option offered to me by Planned Parenthood. My brain hadn't yet clicked over to a viable comprehension level of what an amazing opportunity it could be for all involved. All the pieces fell into the right place at the right time, even though I'd felt so helpless and unsure leading up to that point.

Digging up the memories now is difficult because I really did heal in a healthy, efficient way, all circumstances considered. My choice for a semi-open adoption was what made that process easier for me. That is, as *easy* as it can be to give another mother your child.

I know without a single doubt that Hannah is where she belongs. I'm proud of my role in getting her there, and I know it was guided by a higher power. Making the decision to write this book meant cutting open those wounds to feel all the feelings again, so I can share the journey with others. I didn't just decide I wanted to do this one day, but I couldn't deny the promptings in my heart to speak out as a champion for adoption.

I have been very blessed to have had a great experience. With every letter I received in the mail from Wayne and Leanne, I was comforted that I had made the right choice. Leanne always said the most tender and thoughtful things about how much she loved me and Hannah. I felt so valued and vital to them. And, Wayne and I have similar personalities. I felt like it was an added treat that he did the types of things I would do someday with my kids. He was the goof ball, always cracking jokes and keepin' it real, and was always so loving.

On many occasions people have said to me how easy I make things look. How naturally success comes to me. What they don't see is the grueling hard work and ridiculous expectations I put on myself day in and day out. Overcompensating for things I see as my own shortcomings. This book is a perfect example. No one made me do it. I just said I was going to do it one day, and I love to show off my incredible ability to do things I say I'll do, even when I am not exactly in the season of my life when writing a book seems like a good idea. I'm running on exactly zero time between two small startup businesses, trying not to strangle my husband, and I can't seem to stop having babies of my own.

Rest assured, this book was not easy to write. It was one of the most difficult, brain-melting projects so far. But, even if this book only touches one heart out there, it will be worth it. Heck, if the only copy ends up on my shelf next to my journal, it will be a victory. I don't think that following the promptings to write this book were in vain. In fact, pushing myself through this when I am eye-balls deep in a busy, unpredictable life has actually been an enormous blessing to me. It has been a true pleasure to reconnect with my 18-year-old me, and see how far my own story has come. And, it has been a delightful topic to touch on with my therapist.

Most importantly, it has filled me with excitement for the future. This story isn't over. It's still going. All of our stories are, and no matter how many times we have screwed up along the way, or lost hope, we can always turn the page and start writing something new.

APPENDIX
A Note about Judgment

What have we become? Why do we let so many outside influences dictate our actions, our beliefs, even the clothes we wear and the way we style our hair? Why do we question ourselves and the way we raise our kids, or how we keep our homes? So many of us are so focused on becoming who we think we are supposed to be instead of honing in on our unique personalities and talents to be the super neat individuals we are meant to be. We become the things that others project on us, and, in turn, we are guilty of projecting onto other people as well.

Knock it off!

I wasn't perfect growing up. None of us were. Getting pregnant in high school and placing my baby is certainly the most significant event from my younger years, but I did plenty of other unexpected things, too. We all did. Some things I never wanted to speak up about. I got drunk once in high school. I can't remember exactly when it was, sometime in the fall of 1998 when I had already been working at "TCBY." I was spending the night at a friend's house, whose parents didn't mind if we drank as long as we were under their roof. Pretty cool, right?! (I was terrified.) The parents didn't stay home for the night; they went on a date or something. But, I just went for the glory.

Everything tasted terrible. But, everyone there was doing it so I didn't want to be the odd girl out. I tried to counteract the horrible taste of beer with pizza, Twix, and Twizzlers. I also mixed hard alcohol in with the experience. If I was going to do this, I was going to DO THIS.

A couple hours into the "party," I became, as expected, very sick and was revisited by all of the aforementioned edibles, in no particular order.

I had to open the yogurt shop the next morning, and it was Saturday, which meant it was delivery day. Totally hungover, I dutifully, though mildly cross-eyed, hoisted case after case of frozen yogurt mix off the roller-ramp that was sticking out the back of the shipping trailer. Each case weighed about 30 pounds, which felt like a hundred, and the sound of boxes being slammed onto the ramp, then being launched down the rollers, making this awful shrieking sound was punishment enough that I didn't touch another drink for many years.

My co-worker, Deborah, showed up and immediately called me out. She was calm and sweet, with creamy pale skin, peppered with light brown freckles. Her shoulder-length strawberry red curly hair bounced as she firmly approached me. She stared me straight in the eyes and said she could tell I'd been drinking the night before. She would help me finish unloading the delivery, but she wasn't giving me any mercy or letting me off the hook for the full day of work ahead of me. Tough love. That's something I can get behind.

Besides the people at that party, who probably couldn't have cared less that I was even there, I think I've maybe told five people about this story. I knew people would judge me. I'd heard people talking about the "party kids" behind their backs. I heard people judging others all the time so there was no question in my mind that I would be the subject of that same scrutiny. Some people who know me well might have just been aghast while reading that story just now. Their mind slipping into that common place of judgment without any specific intent. So, reader, if that was you, you can let it go. It was a long time ago, and it isn't your problem.

Shortly before I shared my story online, we were having the usual Law of Chastity lesson in Relief Society (the women's organization within the Mormon church). It was a gorgeous, sunny afternoon and sun rays were beaming into the mauve and doily-adorned room. The potential for a very comfortable conversation was there, the room was set! Yet, there was some of the usual hemming and hawing, and I finally snapped. I announced that I would be sharing something online soon, so they may as well hear it from me in person. I told them that we have to stop being so timid about the subject of chastity. We need to cut to the chase and have some real talk!

We can't rely on children and youth being taught all the nitty-gritty details by an annual church lesson, especially when it barely scratches the surface. We need to own it as adults and parents, not pass it off to church leaders, or health class "sex ed" talks in junior high, and we absolutely should not leave curiosity to find information on the Internet. Talk about mixing up love with lust and derailing all of the sacred beauty of intercourse by twisting it into a dark, seductive, filthy ritual available for a quick, disconnected fix any time, and, thanks to smartphones, anywhere.

After class ended several women approached me and shared with me their relief that I had spoken up. Some shared with me that they were adopted, or have adopted children, and others just thanked me for sharing. But, sure enough, one woman made her way over to me, leaned over and patted my knee saying, "We had *that situation* in our family," and kept walking. I honestly don't think she realizes that it is that EXACT tone that made me hide my pregnancy. <Insert head implosion here.>

When I took my story of adoption public that September 2015, just before my birth daughter's 16th birthday, I was flooded with support. I received many messages from people who said how sorry they were for what I went through on my own.

I also got messages from some of my closer friends who had actually known about the baby shortly after she was born (thanks, Brent), and they had felt so sad for me and so guilty for knowing all these years without saying anything. What?! These are people I'd seen many times over the years, and they never mentioned that they already knew. Talk about awkward and burdensome for them to feel like they were keeping MY secret a secret from me. Sigh. There was no reason to wait for 16 years when I finally popped the cork on it to the general public, but that is what people do. They thrive on secrets, and experience some sort of communication breakdown where talking about real things is incredibly difficult.

Sadly, the people who were the most awkward about it, the people who just as quickly wanted to move onto another subject and have fun with goofy ol' Megan instead of talking about a serious subject, were my Christian friends.

It all comes down to judgment. Yeah, it's hard to talk about real issues, with real people, because our idiot nature makes us evaluate the situation and compare ourselves to what other people have done. It makes us feel better if we can say, "Well, I've never done that. I never partied in high school. Tsk."

I hate to think I was so impressionable that I might have let someone else's advice dictate my decision, but, the truth is, I really do trust people and assume that their opinions are valuable. I take what people say to me as face value and don't question their logic behind it. Nor would I ever expect anyone to tell me something without a genuine care for my best interest at heart. But, here is a thought makes me shutter: What if I had told people, and I got sent away to that pregnant housing situation in Utah where they send all the "bad" Mormon girls to hide the shame it would have put on the family? Yikes. I've heard some pretty horrible stories about people who get shunned and tucked away, out of sight, out of mind, by their own family and it disgusts me.

I had such a high level of expectation of judgment that I only really felt safe sharing my story after I EARNED my stripes. I needed to feel like I had put in an adequate amount of time busting my hump at every job and project I have ever touched, always pulling more weight than I needed to in order to prove myself to anyone and everyone around me. When I finally wrote my blog entry then clicked the post button on Facebook, I braced myself. This story is such an important part of my life, and I'd felt it was important for me to share my experience with adoption because of the positive outcome. I wish I hadn't felt the need to "prove" myself all these years, but ultimately, I was and am proud of the person I've become because of this experience.

At any rate, it worked. I don't know if it would have worked as well 10 years ago. There is no way to know, but I got enough comments from people whose "thank you for sharing" notes were accompanied by mentions of my other business and personal accomplishments. So, perhaps, all that work was worth it?

I, like many other church-going people, was taught "Judge not, that ye be not judged. For with what judgment ye judge, ye shall be judged: and with what measure ye mete, it shall be measured to you again." (Matthew 7:1-2) But, I'll be darned if we don't still mess this up, over and over and over, ad nauseam. I don't think it's intentional, but truly the only way to NOT be judgmental is intentionally not to judge. We have to lead every thought with love and accept that we don't need to know every detail of someone's story; to let that be their story and their journey, and to love them regardless.

We must be compassionate to all people. Every day. In all circumstances. Religious zealots can get lost in the word they preach and forget to feel with their heart the love we should have for every living creature on this earth. To love unconditionally, just as Jesus did.

Love the sinner, not the sin.

If it were humanly possible for us to omit judgment from our lives, imagine the freedom that would follow suit for so many people who continue to hide their secrets and shame for fear of judgment. Living alone, as if they are the first and only to sin. What a glorious place it would be if we could take everyone and every experience at face value, and move forward together with it. We all sin differently. Some things are private, some are easy to detect on the outside. Some only harm the person making that choice, but far more often, the harm affects many other people.

If there were no such thing as judgment, we would have no reason to hide from other people. When we are in the thick of a trial, or actively taking part in a sinful behavior, I think that is when the adversary tries even harder to keep us there. To kick us while we are down. To make us feel like we are the only person on the planet with this pain.

My wish is that real change can start under our own steeples. If we, as Christians, can walk together with open hearts and open arms into the world and stop looking down our noses, we can begin making real change and converting hearts and spreading the light of Christ.

My prayer is that stereotypes can be broken down and we can love one another, as Jesus loves us. I realize that judgment is everywhere, in and out of religious communities, but for those of us who brand ourselves as followers of Jesus, yet do not show love and compassion to "even the least of these" (Matthew 25:40), we are perpetuating the very hate and negativity that we preach against.

ACKNOWLEDGMENTS:

I have typed, and deleted, and retyped this section several times so far, and am overwhelmed at the thought of how many people I should thank.

Initially, I want to thank my Heavenly Father for prompting me to share this story with the world, however, at the moment, I don't *feel* particularly thankful because I've never in all my life been this exhausted, physically and emotionally. This is one of those difficult growing experiences, and I'll be grateful when the book is done and in print. I will, no doubt, look back on this time in my life (if I live through it) with fondness and gratitude for the growth that came with it.

I want to thank Leanne for following similar promptings, along the same timeline, of sharing positive stories of adoption. She is a great partner in advocacy, and an amazing mother.

Thank you to my mother and step-father for raising me to be confident and hard-working, and for always encouraging me during life's adventures. Special thanks for the countless hours my kids got to play at their house while I was writing this book and working on my other projects.

I'm grateful for the support and love from my big, awesome family. My siblings are some of my best friends.

My husband, Mike, you get a unique "thank you" here. Things have been far from easy, and it will take a miracle for us to get on, and stay on the same page in life. The good news is, I believe in miracles, and, with God, anything is possible. Despite the trials, I don't know if I'd go back to try and change anything in our journey. There is a plan for us, even if it wasn't what we thought it would be. I'm grateful for the lessons I've learned so far, and hope you are too. I pray that our story going forward will be one that we are proud of. Our children adore you, and I'm thankful for your help with raising them.

To my young children who inspire me to be a good person, and who treat me like I'm the most amazing human on the planet, thank you for filling my world with joy and laughter. Your radiant personalities definitely cut you slack when you break my jewelry, get your earwax on my earbuds, and spill nail polish onto the carpet.

Thank you, comedy, for letting me be kooky and creative. I'm grateful for the therapy you provide me, the business vessel you afford me, and for the world of possibilities you have opened for me to perform on stage. I'm thankful for your ability to make tough topics more palpable, for the connectivity that you bring to people through laughter, and for your simplicity in things like my 3-year-old's disjointed "knock-knock" jokes. I will remain loyal to you and your capabilities until the day I die.

And, to Hannah, the first person to steal my heart and captivate my soul. I'm grateful for the lessons I learned at a young age about life and love and mistakes and redemption. You gave me a purpose that continues to serve me every day. You make me laugh and cry (usually simultaneously) and keep my world in perspective. I'm grateful for our special connection. It's a true pleasure being your birth mother.

AUTHOR BIO:

An Idaho native, Megan Bryant is a comedian, entrepreneur, and inspirational speaker with an empathetic gift for activating truth. Though Megan has been a wife for 15 years, she is still learning just what it means to be married to her husband Michael. As the birth mother of four children, and mother to three young children (with a fourth on the way), Megan experiences both the highs and lows of motherhood. She would love to invent silent packaging for snacks, so she can eat her Oreos in peace while hiding in the pantry.

CPSIA information can be obtained
at www.ICGtesting.com
Printed in the USA
FSOW02n1922160917
38555FS